WALTER CARROLL
The Children's Composer

WALTER CARROLL

WALTER CARROLL
The Children's Composer
ANTHONY WALKER

Forsyth 1857

© Copyright 1989 Forsyth Brothers Ltd.

All rights reserved. No part of this publication may be reproduced, stored in a retrieval system, or transmitted, in any form or by any means, electronic, mechanical, photocopying, recording or otherwise, without the prior permission of Forsyth Brothers Ltd.

First published 1989 by Forsyth Brothers Ltd.
126 Deansgate, Manchester M3 2GR.

Paperback ISBN 0 9514795 0 4

Photoset and printed by
Halstan & Co. Ltd., Amersham, Bucks., England

For Ida Carroll

Illustrations

Frontispiece   Walter Carroll

1. Dr. Walter Carroll in his academic robes 1900.
2. Walter and Gertrude Carroll with their daughters Elsa (left) and Ida (right).
3. The "Nymphs and Shepherds" choir after making their historic recording on 18th June 1929. Walter Carroll stands with the choir conductor Gertrude Riall, Sir Hamilton Harty stands to the right of the rostrum.
4. The Walter Carroll memorial window in the musicians' chapel of the Church of the Holy Sepulchre, High Holborn, London.
5. W. Heath Robinson created superb cover designs for many of the Walter Carroll music books. This is the cover of "The Countryside". Arthur Rackham and Charles Folkard also contributed designs for the series.
6. "Forest Fantasies" cover design by W. Heath Robinson.
7. "River and Rainbow" cover design by Arthur Rackham.
8. Four covers from todays albums.

Foreword

I am delighted to take this opportunity to place on record my sincere thanks to the author, Anthony Walker, for producing such a detailed and authoritative account of my Father's life and work. My sister, Elsa, and I have welcomed him to our home over the past three years and given him the opportunity to study manuscripts, photographs, original letters and other material which have helped to build up a picture of the man who loved children and devoted his life to bringing to them a joy of music and an appreciation of the arts.

All this, and more, is expertly laid out in the author's text and needs no explanation from me. My wish is to praise his efforts and to hope that many of the millions who use, or have used, Walter Carroll's piano pieces will be interested to know how it all happened.

Ida Carroll
Manchester 1989

Acknowledgments

MANY people have willingly given help in the preparation of this book. The enthusiasm with which they have supplied information and verified details is a tribute to the esteem with which Walter Carroll is remembered.

I wish to record with gratitude the assistance and kindness shown to me by Miss Ida Carroll, former Principal of the Northern School of Music, and her sister, Miss Elsa Carroll, who unfailingly responded to my requests for access to source material concerning their father.

I should like to thank Dr. Alex Robertson of the Faculty of Education, University of Manchester, who supervised the original research, for his interest and encouragement. My thanks are due to Anthea and Robin Loat of Forsyth Brothers for their constructive comments, and to Ian Taylor of Forsyth Brothers for his help at every stage in the preparation of this book. I am indebted to Bernard Starrs and John Turner who kindly read, and made useful criticism of, the final drafts of the manuscript.

In different ways I have received generous assistance and advice from the following:
Miss S. M. Alcock of the Incorporated Society of Musicians.
T. Anderson of E.M.I. Records.
B. Axcell of Novello and Company.
Miss C. Bass.
B. A. Braley of Stainer and Bell.
Reverend W. S. Brown.
Miss S. Burton of Manchester Teachers' Centre Library.
M. Callaghan.
D. Chapman.
B. Cryer, General Adviser (Music) to Bradford Metropolitan Council.
J. Cutler of Kerr's Music Corporation.
J. H. Faux.
G. Fisher.
V. Fox, Senior District Inspector to Manchester Education Committee.
Reverend Sister Frances.
S. W. Freeman of Novello and Company.
P. Green of Sherratt and Hughes.
Mrs. E. Hall (née Jamieson).
A. Hodges, Librarian of the Royal Northern College of Music.
R. F. Jarman, General Secretary of Manchester Y.M.C.A.
J. Kinsman.
K. E. Kitchen, Registrar of the University of Manchester.
Miss D. C. Manley.
H. O'Brien.
Miss D. Pilling.
K. Roberton of Roberton Publications.
S. Rose.
Miss M. Shardlow.
N. Turner of Curwen and Sons.
Miss H. M. Walsh and the staff of the Henry Watson Music Library.
P. Welton.
J. K. R. Whittle.
Miss I. Wilde.

Finally, but by no means least, I wish to thank Celia, my wife, for her constant interest, patience and sympathetic understanding.

Contents

INTRODUCTION

1. **EARLY YEARS** — *page* 3
   Childhood and background. Musical experience and education. Friends and teachers. An academic career in music. Marriage and family life.

2. **INCORPORATED SOCIETY OF MUSICIANS** — 14
   Origins. Carroll's views on music education, the teacher and the child. Lectures and progressive ideas. Training the imagination.

3. **MUSIC TEACHERS' TRAINING CLASS** — 19
   Foundation in 1907. Methods, organisation and influence. Visiting lecturers. "A new era in music education."

4. **THE ART OF TEACHING** — 26
   An ambition realised. The new course. The trained music teacher. Support from Beecham. A crisis and a new beginning. "Glenluce".

5. **MANCHESTER'S MUSIC ADVISER** — 33
   Britain's first full-time Music Adviser. Carroll's schemes for children's music, inside and outside the classroom. Books and lecture-demonstrations. Harty and the Hallé Orchestra. "Nymphs and Shepherds".

6. **MATTHAY SCHOOL** — 66
   Music Teachers' Association. Hilda Collens. Holiday Courses. Carroll as honorary lecturer.

7. **SACRED MUSIC** — 70
   Choirmaster and director of music at St. James's Church, Birch, Manchester. Sacred compositions.

8. **PIANO MUSIC FOR CHILDREN** — 76
   Carroll's piano teaching editions. Carroll's original piano compositions for children: a new age in the musical education of children.

9. **RETIREMENT YEARS** — 114
   Lectures. *The Enchanted Isle*. Magazine articles. *Music in Life and Education*. Final years.

10. **SUMMING UP** — 124

    NOTES — 129

    LIST OF PUBLISHED WORKS — 133

    BIBLIOGRAPHY — 137

Introduction

IT is difficult to state precisely when the idea for this book came into being. As a child, like countless other children learning to play the piano, I was brought up on the *Scenes at a Farm* by Walter Carroll. My acquaintance with his works was renewed when I taught my children to play the piano; the pieces appeared to have lost none of their value and attraction for young pupils.

In my student days in the 1950s, at Manchester University and the Royal Manchester College of Music, I heard accounts of Carroll from those who worked with him or had been taught by him. I knew, of course, the classic recording of *Nymphs and Shepherds* and the Dance Duet from *Hansel and Gretel* sung by the Manchester Schoolchildren's Choir. When I had the opportunity, in the early 1980s, to undertake a research project for a master's degree, Carroll seemed to be a likely subject, for, surprisingly, in view of the range of his achievements and influence, nothing had been written about him, apart from a few short magazine articles.

Born in Manchester in the middle of the nineteenth century, Walter Carroll spent all of his eighty-six years in the city. He is best remembered as the composer of world-famous piano pieces for children. He lived, however, through striking changes in schooling and in music education. For many years the holder of academic posts at the University and the Royal Manchester College of Music, he became increasingly concerned with the need to train music

Introduction

teachers and teachers in elementary schools, thereby improving children's musical experiences and the quality of their lives. In 1920, at the age of 51, he gave up his work with the talented few to devote himself to the musical needs of the mass of ordinary schoolchildren when he was appointed first Music Adviser to Manchester Education Committee – the first such full-time post in the country. Pioneer work was achieved in schools, during a period of great hardship, led by Carroll and his team of dedicated assistants.

Above all, Walter Carroll was a creative educationist, producing in his short piano pieces a change in music for beginners, awakening the child's imagination through an integration of music, poetry and fine illustrations.

He lived a long life of industry and service with his wife, Gertrude, and their two children, Elsa and Ida, making their home a welcoming place for pupils and friends. In times of change he stands as a forthright champion of the value of music in the lives of children.

This book attempts to present a picture of the man and his achievements.

Anthony C. Walker 1989

chapter one

Early years

Childhood and background. Musical experience and education. Friends and teachers. An academic career in music. Marriage and family life.

IN the middle of the nineteenth century a commercial traveller, Robert Carroll, and his wife, Fanny Wormald, moved from the rich agricultural county of Worcester to the grimy industrial city of Manchester. They had four daughters – Edith, Fanny, Florrie and Jessie. On 4 July, 1869, Walter, their last child, was born at 156 Bury New Road, in the Cheetham district of the city.

Walter Carroll had no privileges of birth, money, or schooling. The Carrolls lived in humble circumstances, the mother taking in lodgers to assist the family income. Their household had no special musical interests, though young Walter showed a liking for music; when he was nine his sister Edith started him off with some piano work.

At the age of fourteen, Walter Carroll left Longsight High School, Manchester. His school workbooks testify to the careful workmanship and precise handwriting which he brought to his studies – qualities that remained with him throughout his long life. He obtained employment at the Manchester textile warehouse of J. N. Philips and Company, learning office-routine, letter-writing and the keeping of accounts. A career in business looked likely.

A critical point in his early life came on Easter Sunday, 1886,

Early years

when Carroll, having for a long time attended Baptist meetings with his parents, went to an Anglican Service at St. Chrysostom's Church, Victoria Park, Manchester. The high quality of the music, the choir and the organ-playing made a great impression on him. He asked the organist, Frederick Pugh, if he could join the choir. After the necessary tests in voice and sightreading, Carroll was admitted, taking lessons from Pugh in piano, organ and harmony. Pugh had been a pupil of Sir John Frederick Bridge, organist at Manchester Cathedral and later at Westminster Abbey. Carroll, a serious and determined young man, was soon immersed in the English sacred choral tradition.

Carroll's life was seriously interrupted by the development of pericarditis when he was seventeen. Assisted by his mother's nursing and encouragement of his musical interests, his health slowly improved and he turned more and more to the study of music. His illness, however, left him permanently weakened and he spent the rest of his life with a damaged heart, unable to engage in physical exercise and being forced to sit and write in a straight, upright position. After such a traumatic childhood experience, his devotion to music intensified, and, notwithstanding his disability, his capacity for hard work would have defied many a fitter person.

On 17 March, 1887, Carroll was confirmed in the parish of St. Chrysostom. Attracted by the work of the church musician, he acted as librarian and composed church music for the choir. Soon he was serving as deputy organist and assistant choir trainer to Pugh, who took much interest in his talented protégé. Carroll joined the Hallé Choir, which brought him into contact with a wide field of choral music and gave him additional valuable experience in part-writing and formal design, harmonic progression and the choral repertoire, especially the works of Handel and Mendelssohn. The *Requiem* of Brahms struck him deeply; after his first hearing of the work he went home and tried to play it from memory.

Pugh had a major influence on Carroll's career. He wrote of his young pupil in a perceptive testimonial letter: "He is possessed of considerable ability and shewed great tact and judgement in his

Early years

management of the choir, being particularly successful in training the boys."

Tuition in advanced music theory at this period was provided at Owens College, which had gained University status, as part of the Victoria University of Manchester, in 1880. The classes were taught by Henry Hiles, a leading Manchester musician, composer, organist and author of books on music theory. Carroll's music studies received an impetus when Pugh advised him to attend Hiles' course. When Carroll joined, twenty-one students were registered. At the end of the first year Carroll was the top student and was awarded a Hargreaves Musical Scholarship, with a value of £15. In the second year he came second and in the third he again won the scholarship.

In the absence of a Music degree at Manchester, Carroll entered, in 1891, for the external Mus.B. degree of the University of Durham. This was the first year of the Durham examinations; he was among eighteen successful candidates.

Meanwhile, Owens College had founded a Day Training College for Teachers. Its course extended over three years in order that students might study for a degree and engage in professional training. Masters of Method were appointed to lecture on the theory of education, to arrange and supervise school practice, to organise reading and recitation classes and to teach some academic specialisms.

On 1 July, 1891, Carroll received a letter from the Principal of Owens College, informing him that the College had appointed him as Singing Master at an annual fee of 50 guineas. Carroll, aged 22, had been recommended for this post by Hiles. Carroll delivered weekly lectures on basic music theory, with studies in staff or tonic sol-fa notation, to students in the first and second years.

In 1892, Carroll was appointed organist and choirmaster at St. Clement's Church, Greenheys, Manchester, although concern over his health caused him to give up the post after three years. At this period he composed some church music and piano pieces. Among the latter were two sonatinas published in 1892 by Forsyth Brothers of Manchester, commencing a long and close partnership that was to

Early years

have a vital place in the history of piano music for children.

On 13 January, 1892, he completed a full-scale piano sonata in C minor. This unpublished, four-movement work reveals influences from Haydn and Beethoven. It has a fluency of keyboard writing and, particularly in the finale, a dexterity of contrapuntal writing and wealth of melodic ideas possibly derived from his study of the works of Mendelssohn.

Among the many German immigrants attracted to Manchester in the nineteenth century was the pianist and conductor, Charles Hallé. One of the foremost musicians of his time, numbering Berlioz, Chopin, Liszt, Mendelssohn and Wagner among the great composers he had met, Hallé was instrumental in placing Manchester in the forefront of British and European musical performance. He had founded the Hallé Orchestra in 1858. Now in his early seventies, he was appointed Principal of a new conservatory, which was to open in 1893 as the Royal Manchester College of Music. It was to award a performer's diploma following a course of three years' full-time study. Hallé set about recruiting the finest staff, from home and abroad.

On 27 May, 1893, when Carroll had held his post at the Day Training College for less than two years, Hallé offered him the post of lecturer in harmony and counterpoint at the new institution. Teaching began on 3 October, 1893, when 76 students were registered. Carroll gave the first lecture, commencing a long and fruitful period in his career. Most of the staff were paid 7s.6d. per hour. Carroll, assistant to Hiles, appointed Professor of Harmony and Counterpoint, was paid 5s. per hour. He was one of the youngest members of staff. Within a few years he was also lecturing in composition and history of music.

In 1894, the Victoria University of Manchester established a Mus.B. degree; Carroll entered for the course and passed the final examinations two years later. By this time he was advertising in the musical press as a teacher of harmony and counterpoint by correspondence, and expanding his private teaching practice. He recorded that his first piano pupil began lessons on 26 October,

Early years

1888. From that date up to 1920 he taught privately 382 pupils in piano or harmony, with some voice and organ pupils. He must have possessed distinctive and convincing gifts as a teacher: by 1905, no fewer than twenty-seven of his private pupils had gained the degree of Mus.B. or Mus.D. at the universities of Durham and Oxford.

During the closing years of the century, whilst engaged in his pioneering work at the Day Training College and the Royal Manchester College of Music, Carroll was not neglectful of advancing his own qualifications. In 1900, he became the first to gain, by examination, the degree of Mus.D. from Manchester University.

Two educational booklets were issued by Carroll during this period – *Advice to Students Preparing for Examination in the Theory of Music* (1894) and *Manchester Time and Tune: Exercises for the Use of Singing and Harmony Classes* (1900). They were the first in his series of materials for educational purposes. Throughout his long career he produced similar publications across the entire age-range from infants to advanced students of music.

Gertrude Southam became Carroll's wife in 1896. Like the Carroll family, the Southam family came from the Midlands. Walter and Gertrude Carroll made their first home close to the University, at 188 Upper Brook Street, where Elsa, the first of their two children, was born on 6 October, 1898. Shortly afterwards, they moved to 17 Lansdowne Road, West Didsbury, where Ida was born on 1 December, 1905. The two daughters were educated at Ashfield School, a private kindergarten in Didsbury, and then at Manchester High School for Girls, which at that period was situated in Dover Street, near the University.

Both daughters have made a distinguished contribution to the life of the city of Manchester. For many years Elsa Carroll was clerical supervisor to the Northern Universities Joint Matriculation Board and took a leading part in the Girl Guide movement. Ida, inheriting her father's dedication to music, followed in his profession and became a music education specialist. In 1958, she was appointed Principal of the Northern School of Music and played a major part

Early years

in the establishment of the Royal Northern College of Music in the 1970s.

At the turn of the century Sir John Stainer, Government Inspector and composer of the celebrated oratorio, *Crucifixion*, wrote, concerning Carroll and his work at the Day Training College, that "the fully competent teacher accomplishes much excellent work in the limited time at his disposal." (1)

In the 1900–1901 session, the men's and women's classes were combined for the first time, giving the advantage of four-part music in each class. In 1902, the College established a small elementary school and kindergarten, endowed by Sarah Fielden, one of the great benefactors of Manchester University. Grand-daughter of the Reverend John Yates, a Congregationalist minister credited with founding the first non-denominational elementary school, she married into a prominent family from the mill-town of Todmorden. Her generosity enabled the University to open a demonstration school where new methods of teaching could be investigated and practised.

Mrs Fielden was supported by Sir William Mather, Chairman of the Manchester engineering firm of Mather and Platt, who had a great interest in the work of Frederick Froebel, the German educationist and founder of the kindergarten in which nursery pupils learnt through their own play activities and in which music occupied a place of high value. German teachers living in the Manchester area had helped to found the first Froebel Society in the country in 1873. Mather became Chairman of this society; Walter Carroll, influenced by the child-centred ideas of Froebel, used the Fielden School for the purpose of demonstrations in teaching singing to children.

In the 1904–1905 session, 17 men and 15 women were enrolled in Carroll's first-year class. During the Lent term, extra classes were created for second-year students only, having special reference to the teaching of singing in schools. Carroll was now joined by Thomas Keighley who had been among the early students at the Royal Manchester College of Music. For some years their careers

Early years

were closely interwoven. A few months younger than Carroll, Keighley, a composer of choral music and several music treatises, was organist at Albion Congregational Church, Ashton-under-Lyne from 1898.

In 1904, Henry Hiles, aged 77, retired from his posts at Manchester University and the Royal Manchester College of Music. Carroll was appointed to succeed to his lectureship at the University, the University Registrar confirming the appointment:

> "21 July, 1904
>
> Dear Dr. Carroll,
>
> I beg to inform you that you have been appointed Lecturer in Harmony for three years as from 29 September next, at a stipend of £25 . . .
>
> Yours sincerely,
> EDWARD FIDDES"

The Dean of the Faculty at that time was the Russian violinist, Adolf Brodsky, Principal of the Royal Manchester College of Music since the death of Hallé in 1895. In April 1904, Brodsky had tried to persuade Elgar to become Professor of Instrumentation and Composition at the College of Music when Hiles retired. He offered the post to Elgar in a letter, Manchester University offering a similar post in its Faculty of Music:

> "In Dr. Carroll we have a very good and experienced teacher in harmony and counterpoint who will be proud to prepare the students for you." (2)

Elgar, however, did not accept the posts, taking up the Chair in Music at Birmingham University. Carroll succeeded Hiles as member of the Board of Professors at the College. Three months later, Hiles, to whom Carroll had owed so much, formerly as a pupil and latterly as a colleague and friend, died. Carroll, now aged 34, held three influential posts in the field of music education, at the Day Training College, the Royal Manchester College of Music and the Music Faculty of Manchester University.

Early years

Carroll resigned from the Day Training College in 1909, on his appointment as Professor of the Art of Teaching at the College of Music, but "his work will always be honourably associated with the fortunes of the Department of Education." (3) The principles and methods which he had developed during his seventeen years there were now carried over to the College of Music, reaching greater numbers of students.

In addition to its performer's diploma, the Royal Manchester College of Music had established a teacher's diploma in 1896. In the early years of the twentieth century, a decision was made to review these qualifications. A sub-committee of professors was created, including Carroll. A new scheme of classes for the teacher's diploma was recommended, to include a short course of practical demonstration lessons for final-year students in which each candidate was to take a leading part. Candidates were also required to sit a paper in the art and principles of teaching, utilising the experience gained in the course of demonstration lessons. Other recommendations which were accepted included the provision of a lecture each term on the principles of teaching, to be delivered to all students, in preparation for the teacher's diploma. All students were to be given a practical knowledge of how to teach elementary pupils. Each candidate for the teacher's diploma had to be ready to deliver a specimen lesson for the examiners, and answer verbal questions on teaching.

The new emphasis on the requirements for the granting of the teaching diploma was largely due to the influence of Carroll on the small sub-committee. His main concern was always in the teaching of music rather than the performance. Although a talented organist and choirmaster, he could not be regarded as a performing artist; he was not a highly-skilled performer, unlike the majority of his contemporaries on the staff of the College, and played very little during lectures or lessons.

The Royal Manchester College of Music had from the start a commitment to the training of brilliant performers to take posts eventually as soloists, ensemble players and members of orchestras

Early years

and choirs. In this field it had rapid and remarkable success. However, the early years of the twentieth century revealed not only a furtherance of the practice and skills of performance in music, but also a growing concern with the training of music teachers. Carroll rapidly became a leading figure in these developing areas of music education.

Carroll held his lectureship in the Faculty of Music at the University until 1920. Throughout this period he served as Internal Examiner for Degrees and Secretary to the Faculty, of which Henry Watson, founder of the famous Manchester music library, was a member. At the Board meeting on 23 November, 1909, Carroll was elected Dean of the Faculty, a position he occupied for two years. He served another two-year period from 4 December, 1917.

The early years of the century saw the composition of much of Carroll's choral music, some of it for educational purposes. His chorale, *Sleep Thy Last Sleep*, was dedicated to the students of the Day Training College.

Three more of his educational booklets appeared in the early years of the century. Two of them – *The Study of Music* (1904) and *The Teaching of Music* (1906) – were transcripts of lectures he had delivered at the College of Music. A booklet, *Notes on Musical Form* (1906), was dedicated to his students at the College of Music. Carroll viewed it as a short introduction to standard works on the subject. Republished in 1926, it provided a useful summary of definitions and revision material for students preparing for examinations.

These early educational booklets were designed for advanced pupils, student teachers and those already teaching. From 1906 Carroll's publications reflect his increasing determination to improve the training of music teachers and the musical education of children.

Although Walter Carroll suffered all his life from a weak heart, he did his best to disregard it. A delicate boy and never physically strong in his adult years, he found it difficult to stoop and never joined in outdoor games such as football and cricket. He was a fine chess player, and good at billiards and cards, but never gambled.

Early years

A little below average height, Carroll was slender in physique. He had a quiet manner and a shy disposition. Gertrude Carroll was quite the opposite to her husband in build, interests and temperament: a big, strong woman, she loved looking after the household and was always there to care for their two daughters. To young visitors she appeared somewhat intimidating, but, on closer acquaintance, she proved to be both warm and sensitive.

Carroll had his own study in each of their homes, containing a fine Blüthner grand piano and a large and varied library. Among his favourite authors were John Galsworthy and Hugh Walpole. He took *The Manchester Guardian* and the monthly music journals *The Music Teacher* and *The Musical Times*. Though very much a Liberal at heart, and interested in world affairs, politics were rarely discussed in the home. His work routines and privacy were strictly respected, the two young daughters being forbidden from entering his study, and thereby interrupting him, when he worked or taught at home. In the words of Ida: "We never sat round the fire and talked – Father taught, Mother visited her mother, Elsa did her homework, and Ida amused herself!"

Carroll's musical interests lay firmly with the classics, particularly the great triumvirate of Bach, Beethoven and Brahms. Among individual pieces, a special favourite was the Romance in D flat by Sibelius. He supported the Hallé Choir and Orchestra, especially in the 1920s when they were conducted by Hamilton Harty. Not greatly interested in opera, he nevertheless went to the theatre occasionally – particularly liking the plays of Shaw – and always took his family to the annual pantomime at the Palace Theatre, Manchester.

Carroll lived for his work, even to the extent of rarely playing the piano for pleasure, reserving his keyboard skills for demonstrations to his pupils. His busy life in the early years of the century left little time for hobbies or relaxation: lecturing, teaching and writing filled each day. He claimed that it was far easier to make plans for leisure than to get round to carrying them out. He believed that the teacher needed his spare time for developing his teaching powers, for

Early years

discovering new music for his pupils, and for reviewing and planning his work. However, he did take a complete rest in August, when he avoided all contact with music, a week at Christmas and a week at Easter.

Family holidays included visits to Saltburn-by-the-Sea, Cromer and Tenby, and a few days each year, at Eastertime, spent at Rhyl. From 1911 onwards, the main holiday meant August at Portpatrick, an attractive fishing village in the Galloway area of south-west Scotland, where the Carrolls rented a small house. In spite of his physical disability, Walter Carroll managed to play bowls most mornings on holiday. Not only did Portpatrick become the regular venue for the family holiday, and has always remained so for Elsa and Ida, but it proved to be the inspiration behind Carroll's greatest achievement – the children's piano pieces dating from 1912.

chapter two

Incorporated Society of Musicians

Origins. Carroll's views on music education, the teacher and the child. Lectures and progressive ideas. Training the imagination.

IN 1882, the year in which the Royal College of Music in London was founded, James Dawber of Wigan initiated moves to form an association of musicians. The first meeting was held in Manchester Town Hall on 7 October, 1882, and was presided over by Henry Hiles. The title adopted was *The Society of Professional Musicians*; its primary aim was to provide a representative body of members from the music profession, similar to that in other professions.

At the first meeting, Hiles read a paper, *The Present State of Musical Education in England*, establishing from the outset the commitment of the Society to education in music. The Society was incorporated as an Artistic Association under the Board of Trade in 1892, changing its name to the *Incorporated Society of Musicians*.

This Society rapidly became the most important body of musicians and music teachers in the country. Carroll quickly established himself as an influential figure in its early years. He was elected a member of the Manchester Section on 19 December, 1896. By 1904, he was an official of the Society, holding a post as delegate, from the Manchester Section, to the General Council. He was also one of nine theoretical examiners to the Society.

Carroll's papers presented to the Society from this period

Incorporated Society of Musicians

included *The Profession and Training of Teachers* (1905), *The History of the Pianoforte Sonata* (1905), *The Teaching of Music* (1906), *First Lessons to the Young* (1907), *The Teaching of Music* (1907) and *The Future of the Music Teacher* (1908).

On the opening day of the Annual Conference held in Harrogate in the winter of 1907-1908, Carroll read a paper, *The Training of Music Teachers*. This lecture belongs to the period when he was developing new requirements for the teacher's diploma at the Royal Manchester College of Music and, as we shall see, establishing his own Training Class for Music Teachers. The subject held a central position in his work as music educationist; the lecture was published in 1907. Carroll placed emphasis on two points. Firstly, the Board of Education ought to insist on the teaching of staff notation only throughout all schools. Secondly, he supported the increased use of folk-songs in schools.

Carroll held that the weak link in the professional organisation of teachers of music lay in the private, middle-class teachers. This group had charge of musical training of the young at the critical period of childhood, when technical, intellectual and artistic foundations were laid. He asserted that, with few exceptions, they lacked training in practice and method.

Carroll praised the development and influence of the training colleges, which in the past half century had revolutionised systems of teaching and dominated the field of modern education. Evidently working from his contacts at the Manchester Day Training College, he declared that, compared with teachers of other subjects, the young musician received no training in teaching, stating: "Above all, he must be accustomed to working among children *in order that he may appreciate a child's difficulty from a child's point of view.*" (1)

He advocated the establishment of a Training Class for Music Teachers in every large town, to be under the control, initially, of one or more prominent local musicians, eventually transferring to the charge of one of the diistrict's educational centres.

After describing his own Training Class in Manchester, he referred members to the training colleges and the kindergarten

Incorporated Society of Musicians

system for a proper understanding of the principles of teaching, holding the progressive view that children should be encouraged and helped rather than repressed. He also drew attention to the increased role the government should play in the teaching of music in schools, concluding:

"My experience of this Society is such as to convince me of the great power it possesses in guiding public opinion, and I trust the discussion that takes place to-day may serve to draw attention to a matter which is vitally connected with the educational welfare of the people, and with the future progress of the Art of Music." (2)

On 14 November, 1908, Carroll lectured on *Educational Laws for All Teachers* at the West Lancashire Section meeting of the Society, held in Southport. Once more he stated that it was an established fact that most music teachers were ignorant of the basic laws of teaching, believing that difficulties would pass away with the growth of experience and that, being unable to learn to teach, they would eventually know how when they had taught for a long time. He pointed to the generally accepted view that although teachers of reading, writing, drawing, or painting could be taught how to teach, music teachers either possessed or lacked the gifts of teaching. Carroll held that the cause of this common view lay in the selfish exclusiveness which isolated the musical performer from his musical colleagues. He believed that public opinion demanded the training in teaching for music teachers which other teachers received.

Carroll also spoke of the training of the sensations and emotions, believing that whereas there was much stress laid on the development of musical technique, there was too little paid to the growth of expressive playing and artistic feeling. Part of every child's music lesson should be set aside for the development of the child's power of self-expression, thereby training the child's emotions and imagination as well as technical facility.

A lecture, *The Future of the Music Teacher*, delivered to the Manchester Section of the Society in 1908, contains Carroll's proposal for a music teachers' congress to be held in a large town

Incorporated Society of Musicians

once or twice a year, lasting up to three days, to be centred on discussion of the many problems facing the music teacher. Among his suggestions for discussion subjects were:

1. The need for the appointment of a professional musician to superintend the music of the elementary schools of every large town, together with the formation of a committee to collect evidence and make contact on the subject with the Education Committee.
2. The introduction of violin tuition into elementary schools.
3. Short experiments in teaching music, practical lectures in psychology, and a complete lesson given in each musical subject by an acknowledged expert, followed by discussion.

In December 1909, the month in which he was elected to the post of Sectional Councillor, he gave a short address to the Manchester Section, *The Training of the Imagination: its Place in the Teaching of Music.* Carroll outlined the work of Froebel and then proceeded to trace the training of the imagination in the other arts, particularly in drawing and colouring. Decrying the lack of encouragement for self-expression in music, he put forward three improvements:

1. Teachers should insist that pupils play something from memory.
2. Early attempts at composing or short essays on some pieces of music should be encouraged by the teacher.
3. There should be less emphasis on examinations in music and more time devoted to child-study.

At this point during his fine work for the Society, a series of events occurred which eventually caused him to renounce his membership. In his capacity as delegate to the General Council and Chairman of the Manchester Section, Carroll attended the General Council Meeting in London on 8 June, 1910. It was reported that:

"the question of the election of a President of the Society was submitted for consideration by Dr. Walter Carroll, and, after the matter had been fully discussed, the Council decided that it was desirable, in the best interests of the Society, to elect a President." (3)

Incorporated Society of Musicians

The first President had been the Duke of Saxe-Coburg-Gotha, who held the post from 1893 until his death in 1900. Since then it had been vacant. Against opposition, Carroll urged that the President should again be elected from outside the music profession.

A Special General Meeting was held in London on 28 October, 1910, to consider new articles for the association. At this meeting Carroll regretted very much that, under the new articles, the power of the Sections, who hitherto had a definite veto on the adoption or alteration of bye-laws, would not exist in future. The Manchester Section unanimously supported the views he expressed. A bitter controversy ensued, which culminated in Carroll's resignation from the Society on 14 October, 1911.

Carroll, always a demanding member with a strong sense of vocation concerning the ideas he expressed, severed his links with this eminent society. He had been a member from 1896 to 1911, holding the highest regional and national offices. The Society lost an inspiring lecturer, a tireless and dedicated official. However, seventeen years later, on 17 March, 1928, ties were partially restored, when he lectured once more to the Manchester Section. His chosen topic was that which occupied his life's work: *Music in Education*. In 1976, Carroll's daughter, Ida, a nationally renowned and well-loved professional musician, re-established connections in an outstanding and most intriguing manner: she was elected President of the Society.

chapter three

Music teachers' training class

Foundation in 1907. Methods, organisation and influence. Visiting lecturers. "A new era in music education."

THROUGHOUT 1905 Carroll investigated the subject of music teaching. On 25 November of that year he gave a lecture, *The Teaching of Music*, to the Bolton Musical Artists' Association. He pointed to the small number of fine teachers in the country compared with the large number of eminent performers, and expressed his belief that whereas the performers had undergone a course of training, the teachers generally had begun their work without any methodical training in teaching. His research and work at the College of Music, in drawing up the new schemes of work for the teacher's diploma, convinced him of the necessity for more systematic training. Indeed, for some time he had been requested by music teachers in Manchester and the surrounding towns to consider the feasibility of forming a class to give them instruction in the training of music pupils. Thus, in May 1907, he announced his intention to establish a Music Teachers' Training Class in Manchester.

Any doubts Carroll might have had concerning the success of the class were dispelled in the first month of its inception. Over 80 teachers enrolled in October 1907, and during the session 1907–1908 the total reached 127, the average weekly attendance being 95. The

Music teachers' training class

venue chosen was the Onward Hall, Deansgate, Manchester. Only teachers, and those intending to become teachers, were eligible to join. This pioneering class had an immediate and long-lasting effect on music education in Manchester in particular, and influenced the north-west in general.

The success of this course owed much to Carroll's meticulous preparation and ability in organisation. Individual membership cards were produced and careful arrangements made concerning fees. Carroll established a lending library of new music, on loan from publishers, which quickly established itself as a popular and permanent feature of the course.

The first meeting, with exactly 100 members, took place in the Onward Hall on 17 October, 1907. Carroll gave an introductory address, in which he stated the need for mutual co-operation in the field of music education.

In January 1908, Carroll presented the teachers with a list of questions concerning piano-playing. He concentrated on the simple mechanics of tone-production, different types of touch and movement of the fingers, hand and arm.

Detailed investigations into the entire physical mechanisms involved in playing the piano had already occupied the attention of the London teacher, Tobias Matthay. In 1900, Matthay, Professor of the Piano at the Royal Academy of Music, where he had been a student under the composers, Parry and Sullivan, founded his own school in the capital to advance his theories of piano technique. Laying great emphasis on muscular relaxation, his work culminated in the publication of a classic study, *The Act of Touch in all its Diversity*, in 1903. The leading figure in British piano teaching, numbering Myra Hess among his pupils, Matthay greatly influenced younger teachers such as Carroll.

On 27 February, 1908, Carroll played some pieces by J. S. Bach, suitable for study by elementary pupils. These were included in his collection of 16 pieces, *First Lessons in Bach*, Book 1, published on 1 June, 1908.

In a letter to the members, distributed at the same meeting,

Music teachers' training class

Carroll reminded them that the first session was coming to its conclusion and had given him much encouragement to continue with the work during the following year. Further, he intended to include meetings with the finest visiting lecturers.

Carroll's syllabus for 1908–1909 consisted of a new set of lectures and demonstrations, with special attention devoted to the teaching of the piano and singing. He wrote:

"The whole course will be based on the fundamental laws which underlie all good teaching. The experience of the past session has proved that, in order to grasp the broad principles of teaching, the teacher must go beyond the confines of his own particular subject. He must *compare* his methods, not only with those of his fellow teachers in the same department, but also with the methods of eminent teachers in *other* branches of Music, and of educationists generally. In this way alone can the teacher truly progress." (1)

Specialist teachers were invited for some classes which included voice production and solo singing; all classes were highly practical in nature. Lectures were given on piano teaching by the celebrated German pianists, Max Mayer and Egon Petri, both Professors of Piano at the Royal Manchester College of Music. Mayer, who held his professorship for 16 years, had studied under Liszt at Weimar. Petri, a pupil of the Italian pianist and composer, Busoni, left the college in 1910; among his pupils almost half a century later was the young John Ogdon. Mayer and Petri were among the many formidable virtuosi from the continent who led music in Manchester up to the First World War.

Membership of Carroll's Training Class increased in the second session to 157, with a weekly attendance of over 100. However, in spite of this rapid success, Carroll was not satisfied. In March 1909, every member was sent two extra membership application forms and exhorted to make the Class more widely known.

Among the visiting lecturers during the third session, 1909–1910, was another outstanding figure in the field of piano teaching – Mrs. Annie Curwen – who spoke on 25 November, 1909, on the Curwen

Music teachers' training class

method. Born in Dublin in 1843, Mrs. Curwen achieved much in improving standards in teaching the piano to young children, adopting the educational principles of the tonic sol-fa movement originally applied to the teaching of class singing by her father-in-law, the Reverend John Curwen. A lecturer of particular interest to the north of England was Robert J. Forbes, who lectured on 20 January, 1910, on piano technique. Forbes was appointed Principal of the Royal Manchester College of Music in 1929.

The average attendance in the third session was 98; the total was over 150. By the conclusion of this session it was clear that Carroll's Training Class was achieving a worthy position in the educational life of the city of Manchester. It was stated that:

"A new era in music teaching is in progress, the result of a movement, which, if it had not its inception in Manchester, this city has been the first to put into practical shape, namely, the teaching of music-teachers as distinguished from students." (2)

Carroll's enthusiasm and careful preparation continued, leading him to request journals to advertise his classes for "it is a modest endeavour of my own to raise the standard of music teaching in this district. Financially it is nothing. Educationally it is doing good, and is the only scheme of its kind in existence." (3)

On 26 January, 1911, Carroll lectured on *The Training of the Imagination*, a topic which engaged his attention for many years, and greatly influenced his output of piano-teaching pieces from 1912. He described the imagination as the faculty of forming mind-pictures and argued that, like technique, it can be trained by exercise.

Carroll lectured on *Teaching by Analogy* on 21 November, 1912. He considered that the use of analogy, with its appeal to the child's strong imagination, was of particular use, and that the teaching of singing, notation and expression were greatly helped by the use of analogy. Carroll followed his lecture with two sets of specimen lessons, incorporating his recently-published *Scenes at a Farm*, showing the effect of analogy on the expression of the pupil's

Music teachers' training class

playing.

Membership for the 1912–1913 session was 135. The lending library then included, as well as piano and vocal music, pieces for violin and for organ, and textbooks. In a letter to members, dated September 1913, Carroll laid emphasis on the work involved in the organisation and planning of the course and again stressed the need for an increase in the number of members.

On 4 December, 1913, Carroll gave a lecture on *The Unfolding of Personality*. This lecture was printed, for private circulation only, in 1914. He defined personality as "the (outward) manifestation of the inner self". (4) The teacher revealed his personality in "his eagerness to observe the *good* in the pupil, and to help it to unfold". (5) He lectured on personality several times, in various towns, throughout the 1920s and 1930s. His Nottingham lecture of 1939 was printed as a booklet in 1942. It is a briefer version of the original 1913 lecture.

On 11 December, 1913, in the seventh session, there was an exhibition in the Onward Hall, of children's unaided work from the imagination, consisting of pictures, essays and musical compositions.

The seven sessions of Carroll's Training Class, 1907–1914, had totalled 140 meetings, the average weekly attendance over the whole period being 97. There were only twelve occasions when the attendance fell below 80, the smallest single attendance being 55 and the largest 141. In the session 1913–1914, the membership reached 174, with an average weekly attendance of 117, the most successful numerically during this seven-year period. The majority of members resided within a 40-mile radius of Manchester.

Fifty-one lectures had been delivered by thirty-one speakers including Carroll, whose total of nine was the largest number given by one speaker. Each lecture was followed by a discussion occupying the following meeting, helped by type-written notes on the lecture provided by Carroll for the guidance of the class. Members compared their own experiences and views with those of the lecturer; points of doubt were, in many instances, settled by practical experiments.

Music teachers' training class

The specimen lessons occupied an important place. Fifty were given during the first seven years, some by Carroll, a few by other lecturers, but the majority by members themselves, in all cases followed by a free discussion. Carroll was ensuring that practice kept pace with theory, and the testing of a principle was by its actual demonstration.

Carroll had acted as Chairman at every meeting during the seven years. A low fee of one guinea had been fixed throughout, allowing persons of limited means to join the Class.

The Training Class was held for a further five sessions, until the spring of 1919. The scheme of lectures, discussions and specimen lessons was maintained, with the emphasis still on the teaching of the piano and singing.

The session 1918–1919 was the final one of Carroll's Training Class. With regret, Carroll had to abandon it in favour of the greater claims of his other work. In the final session, he gave the bulk of the lectures, dealing with vocal exercises, notation and sight-singing, and the teaching of musical appreciation to classes. The former direction of the course towards the teaching of the piano and voice to individuals, or small groups of children, had now given way to the training of large classes.

Throughout the whole period of the existence of the Training Class, Carroll was occupied in teaching and lecturing at Manchester University and the Royal Manchester College of Music, visiting schools from time to time, comparing the teaching of subjects, and investigating, with his keen analytical mind, the principles and methods of teaching music in schools.

During the eleven years of the Training Class, hundreds of teachers benefitted from Carroll's work. Carroll had perceived the need for systematic training, including actual contact with the best authorities in the country, and by careful planning and advertising, allied to hard work and enthusiasm, had produced a uniquely successful venture in music education.

Without the support of his wife and daughters, it is difficult to see how Carroll, never robust, could have coped with the hectic round

Music teachers' training class

of lectures, writings, compositions and teaching for so many years. Totally single-minded, he relied entirely on his family for the necessities of life. He never did family shopping nor accompanied his wife or daughters on shopping expeditions. "We shopped for him!" exclaimed Ida. He was, however, sensitive to the needs of his girls; as they grew into adulthood they were given a small dress allowance.

chapter four

The art of teaching

An ambition realised. The new course. The trained music teacher. Support from Beecham. A crisis and a new beginning. "Glenluce".

THE Royal Manchester College of Music was the first of the Royal Colleges to introduce a systematic course of training in the techniques of teaching, including lectures, demonstrations, teaching-practice sessions and compulsory examinations in its teacher's diploma syllabus. This innovatory scheme had been largely the result of Carroll's efforts and was implemented in 1904.

On 31 March, 1909, at a meeting of the College Council, it was decided to found a new department for the special training of those intending to become teachers of music. The College appointed Walter Carroll to head the new department as Professor of the Art and Practice of Teaching.

A cherished ambition of Carroll's was now realised. For many years, at the Manchester Day Training College, the College of Music and the University, he had pressed for recognition of the value of music education. His faith in its development had received extensive coverage at major conferences of the Incorporated Society of Musicians. He had attracted wide publicity at his recently-founded Training Class for Teachers. His overriding aim was stated in 1910:

"Gradually to substitute the trained teacher for the untrained is a work full of glorious possibilities for the art of music. That the Royal

The art of teaching

Manchester College of Music is the first institution to make this training a compulsory part of its curriculum is a fact deserving of the widest recognition." (1)

THE NEW COURSE

ALL teaching diploma students were obliged to attend the new course in their second and third years. Two years' training and examination in the Art and Practice of Teaching were obligatory for the award of this diploma.

Carroll stated that the main aim of the class was to understand the principles of teaching. In each year 27 lectures were given: 8 in the first term, 10 in the second and 9 in the third. At the end of each term, students were to be questioned individually; in the final examination two papers were set, one general and the other special.

Carroll's *Outlines and Lectures for the Art of Teaching* reveal an orderly approach, rich in detail, and with an evident sympathy for the problems facing young teachers. According to Carroll, "to be successful in Teaching, we must regard it, and study it as an art in itself." (2)

The first year of the course consisted of lectures in child-study, pitch, the use of analogy and correlation in music teaching, together with specimen lessons in teaching the piano, violin and voice. In the following year Carroll lectured on personality, training the memory, nervousness in pupils, time and the formation and organisation of a private teaching practice.

Carroll's organisation of the new course was reported by the College Council in 1910:

"The success attending the newly-formed department for the training of music teachers has been most marked, and the Council have every reason, now that the results of the first year's work are obtainable, to be well satisfied with an experiment which is somewhat of an innovation in the equipment of a College of Music. The new classes have been attended with enthusiasm, and any fears that were entertained as to students objecting, on account of the pressure on their time, to an addition to the curriculum, are shown to have been groundless by the exceptionally high percentage of attendances made during the year.

As the great majority of students become teachers immediately after leaving College, the Council were impressed with the need of instituting a course of lectures and demonstrations of a progressive and systematic character, with the express object of fitting them for their future work. That the need for definite training in preparation for this special work is keenly realised is apparent from the fact that many teachers of music, unconnected with the College, have made application to be admitted to these classes." (3)

Carroll must have been gratified to read in the 1913 College Council Report:

"The institution of the Special Department for the training of teachers has been one of the outstanding features of the last decade, and the students have not been slow to appreciate the practical advantages offered to them by this addition to the College curriculum." (4)

About seventy students were in attendance in Carroll's new department in the opening session, 1909–1910. His influence on future music teaching in schools and in private practice radiated through the hundreds of students who attended his lecture-course from 1909 to 1920. Among his students from the earliest years who later themselves became outstanding members of the College staff were the bass Norman Allin, appointed Professor of Singing in 1938, John Wills, appointed teacher of piano in 1921, Dora Gilson, appointed teacher of piano and singing in 1927, and Annie Lord, appointed teacher of piano in 1933.

Carroll, having campaigned for the new department and at last seen its establishment, had to endure opposition throughout the following years. His great self-reliance, single-mindedness and skills in forceful administration, allied to his sense of mission as an educator of music teachers, led inevitably to clashes with colleagues

The art of teaching

and college authorities. He did not always see eye to eye with his colleague, Thomas Keighley, who lectured with Carroll in harmony and composition. He did not approve of Brodsky's autocratic approach to college management. He clashed with Forbes, who, like Carroll himself, was a man of very strong personality. Disagreements among staff in colleges of music are by no means rare occurrences. However, it should be borne in mind that, in spite of their differences, they had all worked together for the good of the College for many years – Carroll from as far back as 1893, Brodsky as Principal from 1895, Keighley from 1898 and Forbes from 1903.

During the period of the First World War events took place at the College which were to be crucial to Carroll's future. In 1915, he was appointed to the College Council. Among the members was Councillor Will Melland, a keen music-lover and supporter of the arts, who had represented Manchester Education Committee since 1912. Melland became one of Carroll's strongest allies and recognised qualities in him which he believed might serve the Education Committee well.

In 1917, Sir Thomas Beecham became President of the College. On 30 November of that year, at the annual meeting, he declared, in typically forthright manner, that a reason why he had accepted the Presidency was that "for the first time in the history of the country, there was a possibility of putting the whole of primary musical education upon a proper basis." (5) He said that the first task for the Royal Manchester College of Music "was that of overhauling and reforming primary musical education in the city." (6) He claimed that this task was the most immediate one for the College, and he hoped to approach local education authorities before Christmas. Further, he stated that, as the Ministry of Education was sympathetic to music, "it was possible to work miracles in the musical education of the country, and of that work colleges with progressive and enlightened ideas could be the focus and the centre." (7) Walter Carroll's views could hardly have been supported more forcibly, in public, by so eminent a musician.

The far-sightedness and shrewdness of Will Melland bore fruit on

The art of teaching

1 May, 1918, when Manchester Education Committee appointed Walter Carroll to a new part-time post of Music Adviser for a trial period of two years. Melland, who sponsored Carroll, was so convinced of the value of the appointment that he offered to subscribe half of the £500 to be paid for Carroll's services. Carroll, aged 49, at the summit of his powers, Dean, Professor and lecturer, turned his attention to the education of the schoolchildren of Manchester. In referring to Carroll's appointment, Beecham said that it was impossible to stress too much the importance of the work that should be carried on in the country's elementary schools, and that musical standards could only be raised by beginning with the school child.

Carroll's dissatisfaction at the College of Music was undoubtedly enhanced in the immediate post-war period of readjustment, a particularly difficult time for musicians of varying nationalities. In 1919, he resigned from the College Council. In April 1920, he accepted the appointment as full-time Music Adviser to Manchester Education Committee, at a salary of £1000 per annum, resigning his academic posts at the University and the College of Music. Born in Manchester, trained in Manchester, his association as member of staff in academic institutions had lasted for twenty-eight years. Aged 51, he renounced this long-standing career serving the musically talented to devote himself to the musical education of the ordinary, elementary school child. As will be shown later, a similar change had already taken place in his musical compositions: from writing choral music for skilled choirs, he had moved to writing piano-teaching pieces for young children.

During his early years as Professor of the Art of Teaching, Carroll and his family lived in Lansdowne Road. In 1911, they moved into *Glenluce*, a large, comfortable residence in Lapwing Lane, Didsbury, a pleasant suburb in the south of the city. With gardens and a spacious attic in which a billiards-table was installed, this house, built to Carroll's specifications, became the permanent family home.

Carroll's study was a sizeable, square and airy room, with plenty

The art of teaching

of windows, on the right of the entrance hall. It was his favourite room, a place for teaching his many pupils, and a retreat where he could compose and write undisturbed. Pupils and visitors waited in the next room off the hall, which was known as the drawing room. In his last years this room became his bedsitting room.

At the end of the hallway and to the left were the family rooms. For many years the Carroll family had domestic help provided by Addie Smith, who lived with them and was always available to help look after Elsa and Ida during their childhood. Walter Carroll, though highly accomplished, creative and meticulous in his professional life, lacked even the most basic domestic skills. According to Ida, "Father only once made his own cup of tea – we used to say that he couldn't even boil a kettle."

Friends from the music profession were frequent visitors; among them were Carl Fuchs and Gustav Behrens from the Royal Manchester College of Music, and the critics, Neville Cardus, with whom Carroll shared cricketing interests, and Granville Hill, a favourite chess opponent. Carroll was a non-smoker and teetotal, but there was always a bottle of port handy for the visits of Tobias Matthay.

Christmas was traditionally a time of celebrations for the immediate family in the Carroll home. The daughters' schoolfriends were invited for special parties on other days, including birthdays. Mealtime routines in the Carroll household were observed with care: breakfast at 8a.m., lunch at 1p.m., and high tea at 5.30p.m. On special occasions the table held good silverware and glasses and fine linen. Correct table manners were instilled into the children.

Though formal in manner and dress, Walter Carroll had a highly-developed sense of humour – more often than not, Ida and her father would see the funny side of life. When she was very young, Ida was taken by her father on several Sundays to churches of all denominations in Manchester: "we always found amusing things such as the time when we attended Morning Service at All Saints and found that the two of us comprised the entire congregation." The Carroll's wedding anniversary was always an occasion for joking; as

The art of teaching

it was celebrated on 12 August (the "Glorious Twelfth") it was a suitable day for Walter and Gertrude to avoid grousing.

chapter five

Manchester's music adviser

Britain's first full-time Music Adviser. Carroll's schemes for children's music, inside and outside the classroom. Books and lecture-demonstrations. Harty and the Hallé Orchestra. "Nymphs and Shepherds".

WITHIN a few years of the passing of the Forster Act of 1870, singing became a compulsory subject in the curriculum of Board schools. Schools were required to prepare a dozen songs and sing a selection to the Inspector. The progress of school music was assisted by Arthur Somervell, Chief Inspector to the Board of Education from 1901, and composer of the once-popular song-cycles, "Maud" and "A Shropshire Lad", at whose insistence the *National Song Book* was introduced into schools. It was during his period of office that some municipalities decided to appoint special officers to superintend music in their schools.

The London School Board had appointed John Evans as organising instructor of singing in its schools as early as 1872. Twenty years later, Evans' assistant, A. J. Cowley, took over the post. By 1908, Cowley had retired, and the London County Council decided that a successor ought to be appointed without delay. John E. Borland was appointed; he held the post until 1926. However, it only became a full-time post in 1920. Other local education authorities which devoted special attention to music education in the period immediately following the 1914–1918 War were Aberdeen, Birmingham, Bradford, Glamorgan, Glasgow, Sheffield

Manchester's music adviser

and Stoke-on-Trent. None undertook the task of developing music in elementary schools more thoroughly, nor presented the results more clearly, than Walter Carroll at Manchester.

Carroll commenced his new post with characteristic determination and careful organisation. His first task was to devote three months to making personal contacts with the teaching staffs, to assess their skills, their weaknesses and difficulties, gaining their interest and assistance in deciding on the type of courses to be offered to them. He visited twenty-eight schools during this preliminary period, to assess existing conditions prior to reform, assuring Manchester Education Committee that

"Music in the Schools, if endowed with fresh life and enthusiasm, will become one of the greatest factors in Education because of its appeal to the sense of what is beautiful and true, and its unique influence on the unfolding personality of the child." (1)

LECTURES ON THE TEACHING OF SCHOOL MUSIC

CARROLL'S programme for the reform of music in Manchester schools was presented to the Education Committee in September 1918, approved and put into effect without delay. He established a series of lectures, free of charge, beginning in the same month, to occupy the winter months, for the staff of Manchester Education Committee schools. Attendance was optional. The only available time was from 4.30 to 6.30p.m., at the end of the school day. Carroll's plans were based on a lecture – schedule of two hours a week, to include singing and voice work, rhythm and ear-training, sight-singing from staff notation, songs, rounds and partsongs.

The response to Carroll's scheme was immediate and overwhelming. Within a few days, 918 teachers, out of a total force of 3326, had been accepted for admission to the lectures. Because of the numbers, it was decided to give each lecture three times, to classes of 300 in each. The venue chosen was Onward Hall, where so many of Carroll's Training Class meetings had taken place. As in his earlier series of lectures, each teacher was presented with a printed summary on leaving the lecture-room; graded lists of songs suitable for school use were also issued.

The series of lectures was planned in three courses, each consisting of eight lecture-demonstrations spread across three years. During most of the lectures, model lessons were given to a class of schoolchildren, by Carroll, followed by questions and discussion. These lessons covered voice-training, reading from the stave and other aspects of vocal music.

In 1919, there were 1166 new applicants for the first-year course, so that, in just over a year, half the teachers of the Manchester Education Committee were in attendance. Carroll reported that, by December 1920, since the foundation of the lectures, 2466 teachers had attended, two-thirds of the teaching staff. By 1925, the total number enrolled for at least one year had reached 3376; of these, 2070 had attended for a second year and 1455 for a third year. Owing to the remarkable response from the teachers in the initial years of the scheme, and their continued interest, the lectures on school music became a permanent feature of Carroll's period as Music Adviser. By 1930, when the scheme had run for thirteen consecutive years, 9721 teachers had attended for at least one year.

The aim of the scheme was "to develop a steady growth of the appreciation and practice of good music in the Elementary Schools". (2) In order to carry out his scheme, Carroll listed several factors which he considered essential or desirable:

"(i) A curriculum which recognises three main objects of musical study – To perform well.
> To listen well.
> To utilise well.

(ii) A teacher whose knowledge of the subject is adequate, and who possesses the power of developing self-expression in the child.

(iii) A period of time sufficient for the needs of the subject.

(iv) A well-graded scheme of work.

(v) A good piano, kept in repair and regularly tuned.

(vi) A link between music and other subjects; for example –

Songs and speech.
Songs and history.
Rhythm and physical movement.
Hymns and the scripture lesson.

(vii) A development of the sense of what is best in poetry and music by a wise choice of songs for school use.

(viii) A school's choir of specially chosen scholars.

(ix) A school's orchestra, drawn from all parts of the city.

(x) A series of concerts and concert-lessons, of good music finely rendered." (3)

Prior to 1918, ear-training and sight-singing were regarded as separate subjects; in Carroll's new scheme they were co-ordinated and interdependent. Singing was now based on staff notation but the principles of sol-fa teaching methods were still used. It was Carroll's opinion that, by employing staff notation in schools, the children were being prepared for instrumental music as well as vocal music, and that by familiarising themselves with a universal script, the children had a means of social contact.

THE DEVELOPMENT OF CARROLL'S SCHEMES

In April 1920, Carroll's trial period as Manchester's Music Adviser came to an end, and he was appointed to the post on a full-time basis. Ten years later, he wrote of the decision to appoint him full-time: "in taking this step the Committee extended to Music full recognition of its importance as a branch of Education." (4)

In 1919, Carroll established a scheme for the teaching of musical appreciation in the elementary schools of Manchester. Staff notation was made an essential feature of school music and song-lists were compiled for the use of teachers. Simple folk songs and national songs were particularly encouraged. In 1920, the use of rounds was developed and improvements sought in the singing of hymns. Teachers were recommended to integrate work in music with scripture, history, geography and dancing. In 1921, the formation of school choirs, to establish standards in singing, was organised, concerts for schoolchildren were utilised more fully, and the Education Committee founded a Music Scholarship of £60 per annum, tenable for three years, on Carroll's recommendation, for young people of at least seventeen years of age. Children with musical talent and promise were enabled to proceed from school to a college of music or university. By 1930, five girls and three boys had won this distinction. Among the early holders were four piano students who took places at the Matthay School of Music in Manchester – Irene Wilde, later to join the staff of the Northern School of Music, Jack Davies, who died at the age of 30, his exceptional promise unfulfilled, Edna Jamieson, the young accompanist to the Manchester Schoolchildren's Choir, and Albert Knowles, later to be répétiteur at Covent Garden Opera.

In 1922, classes were established in speech-training under the direction of Miss Buxton Nowell, who had joined as an assistant to Carroll two years earlier. In September 1922, the first session opened with a membership of 285. Up to 1930, the total number of teachers who had attended reached 1291. The course, lasting one year, consisted of thirty-six weekly lectures, each of eighty minutes, from September to July.

SINGING IN SCHOOLS

IN 1930, Carroll wrote:

"It is in Voice Training that the best results of all have been achieved . . . It is hardly too much to say that, in a few years, a complete revolution took place in this branch of school music." (5)

Improvements in the teaching of class-singing in schools can be summarised under three headings:

1. Voice Training. Carroll recommended the singing of descending scales, the cultivation of forward tone, flexibility in place of force, outward in place of inward thought, and imagination.

2. Songs. Criticising the low standard of material, he urged an increase in good unison songs, based upon staff notation, but with the sol-fa principles and syllables as an aid, the use of simple rounds and descants in place of poor attempts at difficult partsongs, and singing from memory. A good piano, well in tune, was recommended for songs, but he believed that it was necessary only as a means of giving or testing pitch.

3. *Ear-training and Sight-singing.* Carroll's recommendations were based on the necessity of forming an aural rather than a theoretical foundation in this area of study. The use of phrases was preferable to single notes, sung answers in place of written answers and the scale was recommended as the foundation of aural work instead of the chord.

In 1930, Carroll noted that the standard in musical skill of pupils admitted to secondary schooling had been considerably raised by the achievements at primary level. He complimented the teaching staffs on their efforts and co-operation:

"For all these changes in the direction of brighter and more intelligent work great credit is due to the teachers who have endeavoured loyally to put into practice the newer methods which they saw demonstrated in the Lecture Courses." (6)

THE TRAINING OF CHILDREN'S VOICES (1922)

IN 1922, Carroll's booklet, *The Training of Children's Voices* was published. Intended primarily for use in schools, this volume could also be adopted by church choirmasters and individual singers. It consists of two sections, firstly a guide to the teacher and, secondly, a collection of vocal exercises originally compiled for the training of boy choristers.

Carroll draws attention to the harmful custom of associating the child's voice with the scale of C, because "the child's voice lives in higher regions." (7) He defines the average vocal compass of the child of five or six years as approximately a tone above the generally accepted, i.e. the scale of D. From the age of seven to fourteen, there

1. Dr. Walter Carroll in his academic robes 1900.

2. Walter and Gertrude Carroll with their daughters Elsa (left) and Ida (right).

3. The "Nymphs and Shepherds" choir after making their historic recording on 18th June 1929. Walter Carroll stands with the choir conductor Gertrude Riall, Sir Hamilton Harty stands to the right of the rostrum.

4. The Walter Carroll memorial window in the musicians' chapel of the Church of the Holy Sepulchre, High Holborn, London.

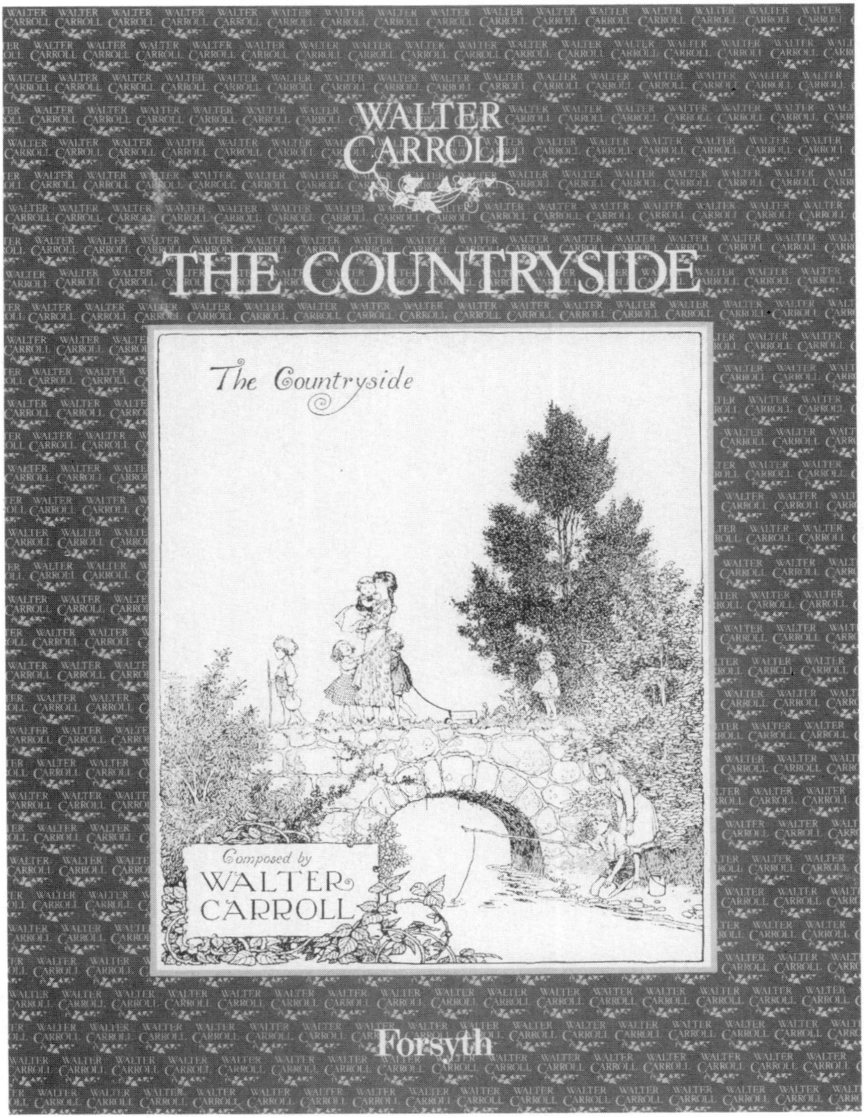

5. W. Heath Robinson created superb cover designs for many of the Walter Carroll music books. This is the cover of "The Countryside". Arthur Rackham and Charles Folkard also contributed designs for the series.

6. "Forest Fantasies" cover design by W. Heath Robinson.

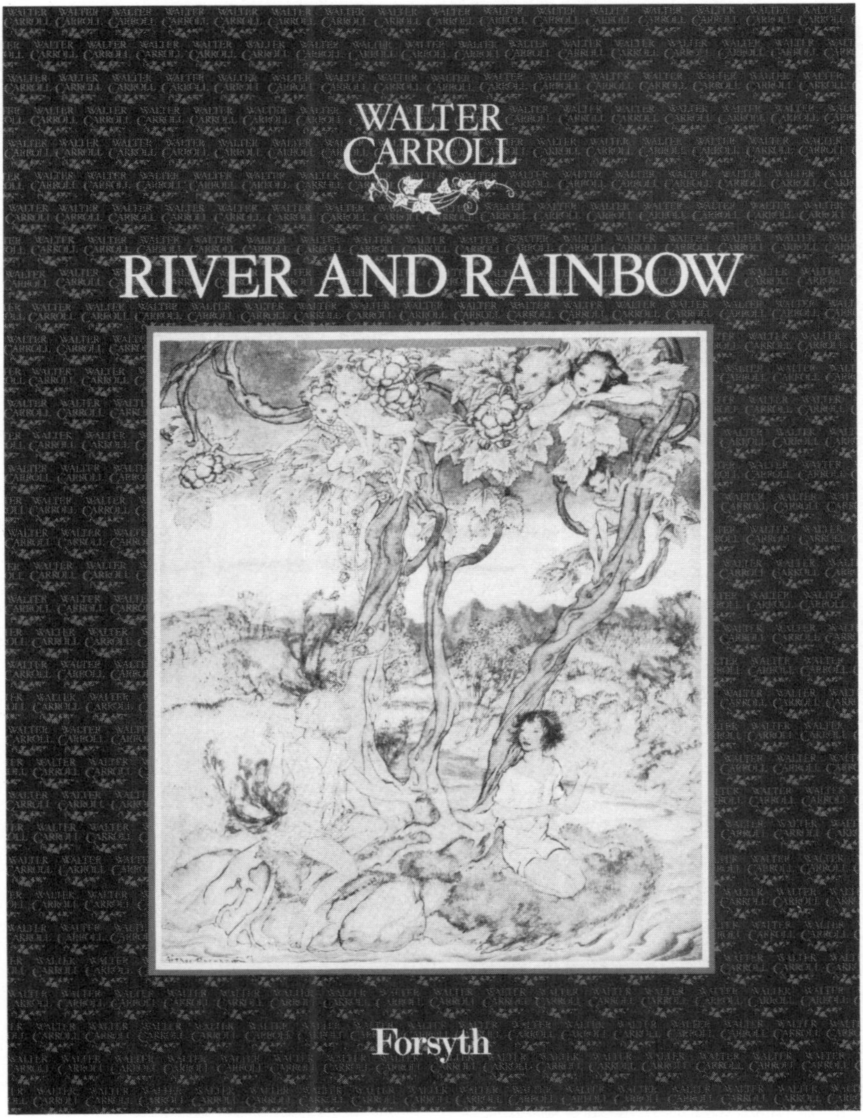

7. "River and Rainbow" cover design by Arthur Rackham.

8. Four covers from todays albums.

is a gradual extension – downwards very little, to B or B flat; upwards a good deal. The eleven-year old is able to sing a top G easily. By thirteen, nearly every child can sing top A or B flat. He stresses that correct training, including the production of forward tone and practice of descending scales, will produce a fine result in the child.

Plenty of vocal exercises are included, intended to be sung from memory, directed by the teacher. The volume embodies Carroll's long experience as a trainer of choirs, students and serving teachers, and reveals an orderly and progressive approach to the subject, yet without sacrificing the qualities of imagination, creativity and enjoyment to the demands of increasing the technique. It put into convenient form the methods which he had built up after experimental research and delivered orally during his lectures.

The Committee of the Music Teacher's Association invited Carroll to address the members at Mortimer Hall, London, on 13 May, 1922, the year of publication of *The Training of Children's Voices*. He chose for his subject *Interpretation in the Choral Class*. He spoke of the words of songs as the basis for interpretation in the choral class, stressing that before interpretation was possible there must be a certain level of technique. Illustrations were provided by eleven songs in varied styles, sung by Gertrude Riall, later to serve as an assistant to Carroll.

CARROLL'S SCHEME FOR THE TEACHING OF MUSICAL APPRECIATION

THE provision of training in more and better methods of teaching singing remained at the core of Carroll's schemes for the development of school music in Manchester. However, the nineteenth-century concept of restricting the curriculum to vocal music alone was, in his view, mistaken.

By the time of Carroll's appointment to Manchester Education Committee, the music curriculum was expanding, aided by the progressive attitude of authorities such as Manchester. Carroll's aim

Manchester's music adviser

was that "a knowledge of the Art of Music which shall extend beyond the limits of the singing class ought to be recognised as an integral part of a liberal education." (8)

Carroll inaugurated the scheme for teaching musical appreciation in schools in September 1919. Manchester was the first local education authority to provide such a regular and systematic course of instruction. Emily Allen, a specialist teacher, was appointed to teach the subject in thirty-six schools; the children in this first group numbered approximately 3000. In January 1920, a second teacher was appointed and in September 1920, a third teacher joined the special staff. One hundred and eight schools took part in the scheme, with at least 9000 children receiving lessons. The specialist teachers appointed to this work, with Miss Allen as senior assistant, were Stanley Grundy and Christie Green. Specialist teachers were appointed because Carroll felt that this instruction could only be given effectively by those with special training in music. Lessons were given once every three weeks to children aged from 11 to 14. Eighty to 120 children were present in each class. The full course was designed to last three years. The general aim was to associate the children with music in its fuller sense, with a prime objective of introducing them to examples of beautiful music from the masterworks. Among the qualities necessary for a successful teacher in this subject, Carroll selected very good pianistic skills and a gift for story-telling as the most relevant.

Lasting about forty minutes, an appreciation lesson included a few brief questions on the previous lesson, a short talk on a new topic, musical illustrations played or sung by the teacher, and experiments in which the children took an active part by humming or tapping out the important phrases.

For the detailed planning and presentation of the lesson, the teachers were left to follow the inclinations of their own personalities. In Carroll's view, a set syllabus for uniform application in an area so dependent on individual temperament would be an obstruction. He felt that a sense of ease and consciousness of freedom were very important to the teacher of

Manchester's music adviser

musical appreciation. Pieces selected for the early stages of the course were usually very short, such as the piano miniatures of Grieg and Schumann. Longer pieces were introduced gradually; the earliest works were generally programmatic.

Occasionally the gramophone could be of use, but, in his opinion, the children soon tired of it and were more interested in the performance of music by the teacher; once more he stressed the force of the teacher's personality, which no mechanical means could effectively supersede. He was always cautious of the use of mechanical aids in the classroom. In his own home he showed a lack of interest in radio and recordings; indeed, he never possessed a gramophone. A far more pressing need, in his view, was the provision of school pianos. Conditions during the 1914–1918 War had badly affected the supply and servicing of school pianos in Manchester. Carroll took a census of all the pianos in 1918, and planned for gradual renovations or the supply of new instruments. He discovered that sixty schools did not possess a piano at all. Piano tuning and repairs were re-organised on a systematic basis. By 1926, all schools had been supplied with a piano.

Carroll publicly expressed his ideas concerning the teaching of musical appreciation at the National Conference on the Leisure of the People, held in Manchester in November 1919. He stated that the recreative life of people is the outcome of early environment and habit, a maturing of interests formed in childhood. He believed that if the Manchester scheme were to be adopted in schools throughout the country, a practical way would have been found to guide the tastes and interests of young people, train future audiences for concerts and opera, and create a desire to devote leisure time to music.

In 1920 Carroll was able to report that:

"Many other towns are writing for information, especially in regard to the Training of the Teachers, and the Music Appreciation Courses. It is probable that, up to the present date, Manchester is the only city with *organised* teaching of Musical Appreciation in the Elementary Schools, but there is every indication that other

Manchester's music adviser

Authorities are about to adopt similar measures." (9)

Carroll's lectures to teachers on the teaching of musical appreciation included the following venues:

Blackpool, Stoke, Wolverhampton	1922
Bristol, Mansfield, Southport	1923
Birmingham, Bury, Cannock, Salford	1924
Burnley	1925
Colne, Dewsbury, Nelson, Preston	1926
Bolton, Wakefield	1927
Huddersfield, Rochdale, Wigan	1928
Blackburn, Leeds	1929
Widnes	1930
Nuneaton	1931

On most occasions a class of children were present to receive a typical Manchester lesson. Each lesson contained a programme of musical illustrations, three or four keyboard pieces ranging from Bach to MacDowell, Coleridge Taylor and Carroll himself. Each listening lesson, he advocated, should conclude with the teacher playing or singing a new piece, for attentive listening, without any discussion of its meaning.

CONCERTS FOR CHILDREN

A BROADER policy for the music curriculum in schools in Britain was being advocated by progressive music educators in the early years of the twentieth century. Concerts specially organised for children, frequently with explanatory programmes, revealed a growing interest in training pupils as listeners. Persistent campaigning, particularly by the leading figures of the musical appreciation movement, such as Stewart Macpherson and Percy A. Scholes, caused some more enlightened authorities to move forward. In the forefront of this movement was the municipality of Manchester.

In October 1916, with the support of civic and school authorities, a Children's Concerts Society was formed in Manchester. Its

Manchester's music adviser

committee consisted of private citizens, several of whom were associated with the city's schools. The chairman was Will Melland. Seven concerts were given at 3p.m. on Saturdays during the winter months, the first being in the Houldsworth Hall on 18 November, 1916.

Solo items, ensembles and orchestral music were represented in fair proportions. Each concert was planned around a single idea, with a short explanatory talk on the pieces. Expenses were met entirely by the admission charges; reserved seats for the series cost 3s. 6d. Arrangements were made with the schools, through the Director of Education, whereby several hundred children, from elementary and central schools, were invited to attend at a nominal fee; the gallery was reserved for their use. From 1918 onwards, Carroll was able to link these concerts with his new school music schemes. Although much good work had been done already, he further developed their potential, aiming to reach a larger audience than in previous years. With Carroll's appointment, Manchester Education Committee took a more active part in the promotion of these concerts.

The opening concert of the 1918–1919 season, arranged by Carroll, was transferred from the Houldsworth Hall to the larger Central Hall, with its seating capacity of about 1500. At this concert, Carroll took as his theme *The Voices of the Orchestra*, illustrating it by a mixed voice quartet and an octet of wind players.

The Children's Concerts Society presented its series of concerts, seven in each series, until 1926. Each concert was attended by over 1000 children from Manchester and Salford schools. A syllabus, including the titles of each concert, artists, lecturers and dates was produced at the start of each session. The syllabus included the four reasons why the series was of importance to the child:

"1. The appreciation of Harmony stimulates a desire for beauty.

2. The understanding of Form stimulates a love of order and method.

3. The training of the Ear stimulates concentration, receptivity

Manchester's music adviser

and alertness.
    4. The poetry of Music stimulates self-expression."

1923 witnessed a major event in the musical education of many Manchester schoolchildren. On 21 December, members of the Hallé Orchestra, under their conductor, Hamilton Harty, gave an experimental concert to schoolchildren from Manchester, Salford, Stockport and Stretford, to determine whether the provision of orchestral music at reduced rates for children should be included in any municipal scheme. About 2500 children attended this free concert in the Free Trade Hall, Manchester. The programme consisted of:

Humperdinck,	Overture: *Hansel and Gretel.*
Mozart,	*Serenade for Strings.*
Haydn,	"In Verdure Clad", from *The Creation.*
Tchaikovsky,	*Nutcracker Suite.*
Boughton,	"The Faery Song", from *The Immortal Hour.*
Bizet,	*Children's Suite.*

The two solos were sung by Miss Bella Baillie, the celebrated soprano, later to be known as Isobel Baillie. Harty noted that the children's behaviour was delightful, and that the concert was a highly important experiment in the field of music education.

Thus began a unique association between a world-famous orchestra and its conductor with the schoolchildren and teachers of a northern city and their Music Adviser. In the depressed era of the 1920s, the progressive and enlightened attitude of Harty and Carroll brought about a short, yet concentrated, collaboration without parallel. This culminated in a joint performance and an unprecedented joint gramophone recording in 1929.

In 1924, the Manchester City Council, by a large majority, engaged the Hallé Orchestra for a winter series of six Municipal Concerts. 500 balcony seats were to be allocated to the schoolchildren of Manchester. Admission charges ranged from 8d. to 2s. 4d., with schoolchildren at 6d. each. In this season the Town Hall Committee estimated the deficit at £1000.

Manchester's music adviser

Will Melland suggested that the most important aspect of the scheme was the reservation of seats for 500 schoolchildren. He drew attention to the success of the Children's Concerts Society during the last seven years with its average attendance of 1000 children, nearly all from elementary schools. In particular, he drew the Council's attention to the work of their Music Adviser in the field of music education, stressing the splendid results of the scheme for the teaching of music appreciation.

The Municipal Concerts proceeded, on Monday evenings, in the Free Trade Hall. The response from the children was overwhelming, the 500 special tickets being rationed. A second special children's concert was given on 19 December, 1924, with admission offered free. Presented almost exactly one year after the first experimental concert specially for children, this concert again attracted an audience of 2400 boys and girls, about half coming from the Manchester elementary schools. Carroll reported:

"The concert was the second of its kind given, without charge for admission, by the Hallé Society and these two generous acts have enabled ten children from every senior school in Manchester to visit the Free Trade Hall, and to hear one of the finest orchestras in the world." (10)

For several years the concerts given by the Children's Concerts Society and the Municipal Concerts given by the Hallé Orchestra overlapped; there was no break between the former scheme of 1916 and the latter of 1923. In 1926, the Children's Concerts Society ceased. However, its work and influence had merged into the wider sphere of municipal provision.

As a movement, it appears that the provision of orchestral concerts for children was a post-1914–1918 War phenomenon. Robert Mayer, a wealthy German industrialist living in England, inaugurated, on 29 March, 1923, a non-profit making, privately subsidised venture, *Orchestral Concerts for Children*, in the Central Hall, Westminster. Adrian Boult conducted the orchestra and introduced the items to the young people. The cities of Aberdeen,

Manchester's music adviser

Birmingham, Edinburgh and Nottingham also provided concerts for children.

MANCHESTER SCHOOLCHILDREN'S ORCHESTRA

IN March 1923, Carroll had discovered, after a period of enquiry, that about two hundred children in Manchester elementary schools could play an orchestral instrument. Each potential orchestral player was auditioned, resulting in the formation of a string orchestra of about 50. The players met once a week at Granby Row School, after school hours, under the direction of one of the Education Committee's staff, H. W. Wrigley, Principal of Mill Street Unemployment Centre. The number of children attending the orchestra increased so that in September 1925 it was divided into two sections, junior and senior. By 1930, the collective membership was 70.

The Schools' Orchestra made its first public appearance during a special Education Week in June 1924. A series of events was presented giving parents and public an opportunity to become acquainted with the growing musical activities of the city schoolchildren. The Schools' Orchestra played at a concert held every evening in the Free Trade Hall, and at the Lord Mayor's Reception in the Town Hall, including items by Bach, Boccherini and Schubert.

In 1925, when the senior branch was formed, Stanley Grundy undertook the training. He continued as conductor until 1931, when Archie Camden, principal bassoonist in the Hallé Orchestra, took over the work. Two years later, when Camden was appointed principal bassoonist in the B.B.C. Symphony Orchestra, Eric Fogg became conductor of the Schools' Orchestra. A popular character with the children, Fogg was known to them as "Uncle Eric". He belonged to the same group of broadcasters, from the "Children's Hour" programmes, as the pianist "Aunti Vi" (Violet Carson), renowned in more recent times as a star of the television series,

Manchester's music adviser

Coronation Street.

Following its first public performance the orchestra gave concerts during the following years at various venues, including the Town Halls of Levenshulme and Newton Heath. On 26 March, 1926, a concert was given in the Free Trade Hall at which the orchestra performed. This became the first in a series of Annual Concerts, giving parents and children an indication of the progress being made in music as a central feature of the educational life of Manchester, and having as its main object "to arouse in the child the desire to give pleasure to others, and to use the gift and knowledge of music as a means of rendering public service to the city". (11)

Each year from 1926 to 1935, the Annual Concert, given entirely by schoolchildren, filled the 2500 places of the Free Trade Hall. Several groups of orchestral pieces featured in each programme. Characteristic of the pieces played were the following:

Bach,	Movements from Orchestral Suites 1 and 2.
Walford Davies,	*Solemn Melody.*
Delibes,	*Passepied.*
Grainger,	*Country Gardens*; *Shepherd's Hey.*
Grieg,	Symphonic Dance number 2.
Haydn,	Andante and Minuet from *Surprise Symphony.*
Järnefelt,	*Praeludium.*
Lully,	Minuet from *Le Bourgeois Gentilhomme.*
Mozart,	Minuet and Trio from Symphony number 39 in E flat.
Parry,	*Air and Pastoral.*
Purcell, arr. Dunhill,	Suite, *The Old Bachelor.*
Quilter,	*Country Dance*; *Shepherd's Holiday.*
Rowley,	*Four Dances.*
Stanford,	*Suite of Dances.*

Several dozen young musicians appeared as soloists over the years, among them the pianist Rayson Whalley, later to join the Hallé Orchestra, George Fisher, who played the organ solo in Walford Davies' *Solemn Melody* and then Chopin's Polonaise in C

Manchester's music adviser

sharp minor in the 1931 concert, Myra Scott, noted for her playing of Brahms, and the fine violinist, Brenda Old. Jack Davies played Chopin's Ballade in A flat in the 1926 concert and the same composer's Scherzo in E in 1927.

By 1933, the total of players had reached 96, consisting of 55 in the junior section and 41 in the senior section. Soon after the Annual Concert of March 1933, the Manchester Broadcasting Station invited Carroll to prepare an hour's programme of music given by schoolchildren. On 6 April, from 6.30p.m., a choral and orchestral concert was broadcast from the Piccadilly Studio. This was the first occasion on which the Schools' Orchestra had taken part in a broadcast performance. A similar broadcast took place in May of the following year.

The Schools' Orchestra continued its activities after Carroll's retirement, until the onset of the 1939–1945 War, when it was disbanded owing to the evacuation of schoolchildren from the city.

THE DISSEMINATION OF CARROLL'S SCHEMES

CARROLL'S schemes for music education, allied to his own personal qualities, and the invaluable support he received from Spurley Hey, Director of Education, and Will Melland in particular, combined to create a rapidly growing and effective music curriculum in the schools of Manchester.

In 1920, Carroll reported that many towns were writing for information, indicating that other authorities were about to follow Manchester's example in music curriculum developments. He lectured on the Manchester scheme in Hull in 1920, Altrincham, Burnley, Hanley, Todmorden and Wigan in 1921. In 1922, requests came from thirteen new centres, including Blackpool, London, Stoke-on-Trent and Wolverhampton. Among the visitors from abroad were representatives from the South African Board of Education, Vancouver, Melbourne and the University of Cape Town.

Manchester's music adviser

Carroll asserted that by 1924 his music schemes had been established in all the Manchester schools. Each evening during Education Week of that year, a concert was presented in the Free Trade Hall by pupils from the schools and other institutions of the Manchester Education Committee. A choir of 360 children from the elementary schools provided the basis for each concert. Six such choirs, totalling over 2000 children, performed during the week.

Education Week culminated at 2p.m. on 28 June, with a mass demonstration of music, games, physical training and dancing at the Manchester Athletic Club Ground. The opening item was the singing of songs by massed choirs, conducted by Carroll – one of the few occasions when he conducted in public.

Specimen lessons in the teaching of music appreciation and daily organ recitals were given by Carroll's staff. Morning concerts were given by children from the infants' schools, including a choir of infants numbering 120 voices. At the Lord Mayor's Reception in the Town Hall, the music was provided entirely by children from the city's elementary schools.

On 4 January, 1924, Carroll delivered an address, *The Place of Music in Education*, at the North of England Education Conference held in Blackpool. He remarked on the changing outlook on music in education and on the growing conviction that music was a necessity not a luxury. He noted, too, a return to Greek ideals in the stress on the value of music in the training of character. He argued that, in some degree, the 1914–1918 War had caused a change in attitude: "by cultivating in the people a love of what is beautiful we are taking the surest course towards the elimination of brute force and ugliness of every kind." (12)

To conclude his address, Carroll summed up his aims for the musical education of elementary school children up to the age of fourteen:

"1. A love of good music for its own sake.
2. Good breathing habits.
3. Sweet voice, with forward tone, no breaks or registers.

Manchester's music adviser

4. A sensitive ear for pitch and rhythm.
5. Facility in reading simple tunes from Staff Notation.
6. A large number of good songs.
7. An appreciation of the language of Music as expressed through rhythm, melody, harmony.
8. A knowledge of musical literature through hearing standard works well played."

Carroll spoke, a year later, about the Board of Education, which ten years previously would not consider expenditure on music as justifiable, now giving every music scheme a sympathetic hearing. Moreover, local authorities were now encouraged to propose music schemes. In his view, they had come to realise music education as a national asset.

HANDBOOK OF MUSIC: A COURSE OF WORK FOR ELEMENTARY SCHOOLS (1925)

DURING 1924, when Carroll's schemes for the revised system of music education in Manchester's schools had been in progress for six years, he worked on the production of a Handbook providing the staff of the schools with a statement of aims, syllabus of work, notes on his lectures to teachers and graded lists of songs. Intended as a guide for teachers, enabling them to plan and adapt their own particular work in relation to the overall scheme, this volume was published by Manchester Education Committee in January 1925.

In his Preface to the volume, Spurley Hey wrote:

"The Education Committee have been encouraged by the great developments which have been brought about in the teaching of school music during the last few years, and it is with the object of concentrating teaching effort upon, and of giving an even greater stimulus to, musical training in the schools that this Handbook has been compiled and issued. The Committee look forward with confidence to the continuation of the successful developments of the last few years in the teaching of school music."

Manchester's music adviser

In his Introduction, Carroll stressed the importance of having a clear aim in every lesson and planning the work in relation to that aim. He urged that teachers should teach the reading of music from staff notation to children from the age of seven, and continue it through every grade until the children left school.

A syllabus of work is presented for the entire elementary school. Each age-group has a series of exercises, examples and lesson procedures; he recommends constant revision and practice of songs, exercises and theoretical work, with the teacher performing songs to the children whenever possible. The vocal exercises in this Handbook are all taken from *The Training of Children's Voices.*

Each department in the Education Service was provided with two copies and, in addition, many teachers bought copies for their own use. During 1925, the total number of copies distributed to schools and individuals was about 3250. The reviewer in *The School Music Review* commented:

"The Handbook should be seen, read, and digested by supervisors and teachers throughout the country.

What the Manchester Committee has done we hope all other committees will do in the near future. Not only is the Committee to be thanked publicly for its progressive attitude to music, but it is to be congratulated on having secured the right man to carry its ideals to fruition." (13)

In 1926, Carroll reported that a number of towns, including Batley, Burnley, Bury, Dewsbury, Dudley, Nelson, Preston, Salford, Southport and Wolverhampton, had adopted the Handbook. By the end of 1926, the first edition of 5000 copies was almost exhausted. A second edition was issued in April 1927. By 1930, 7500 copies had been issued, applications coming from Canada, Cape Colony, India, New Zealand, Nigeria, Perth, Rangoon and Singapore. In September 1933, Carroll reported that nearly 10,000 copies were in circulation, and a third edition was being prepared. This third, and final, edition appeared in March 1934.

Manchester's music adviser

Carroll's Handbook was a musical blueprint for other such guides issued by education committees and local authorities. Published by Manchester Education Committee, it represented the philosophy, aims and methods evident in their official scheme of music education.

MANCHESTER SCHOOLCHILDREN'S CHOIR

DURING Carroll's period of development of music in Manchester schools, the first objective was good singing. Under his guidance and encouragement from 1918, small choirs were formed in individual schools, the children regarding membership as an aim and reward for good work in the singing class.

In May 1925, two years after the formation of the children's orchestra and four months after the publication of the *Handbook of Music*, a Manchester Elementary Schools' Choir was founded. This choir, one of Carroll's best-known schemes for music education, began with the formation of two sectional choirs in the northern (Newton Heath) and southern (Longsight) areas of the city. The training of the choir was placed under the control of Gertrude Riall, a new member of Carroll's music staff, appointed in 1923. A petite figure, who occasionally had to climb on a chair to conduct, and was at times frightening to the young children, who labelled her "Shirty Gertie", she had much of Carroll's down-to-earth approach, sharp sense of humour and ability to bring out the best in children. She possessed those rare gifts of personality, musicianship and flair given to the finest choral conductors.

About 150 schoolchildren, aged from nine to fifteen, selected from schools in the district, attended each section. Rehearsals were held for one hour, commencing at 5.30p.m., once a week, from September to March. Rules as to regular and punctual attendance were carefully observed, in spite of the fact that many children had to travel some distance to rehearsals. The training of the two sections was uniform, enabling them to join together for massed singing.

Manchester's music adviser

Gertrude Riall, sharing Carroll's enthusiasm, dedication and capacity for hard work, had already visited schools throughout 1924 and the first months of 1925, to organise the selection and tuition of choir members. The two sections worked hard at vocal exercises, articulation and high voice techniques; the procedure was laborious but it produced a fine result. She led by example, urging the children to project their voices, to direct their sounds towards the windows at the back of the room, with mouths wide open as if holding an orange. She took over the specific training and conducting duties, but under Carroll's overall direction.

Most weeks Carroll appeared at rehearsals, even walking up to individual children, cupping his hand to his ear to listen and check their voices whilst the practice was in progress. He was always neatly dressed in a dark three-piece suit, with white shirt and stiff collar, tie and pin, "forbidding, like a nineteenth-century gentleman". (14) He was precise, strict and highly critical; to some of the children he appeared similar to a Superintendent of a Sunday School. The choir stood in awe of Carroll. When he occasionally conducted he never raised his voice, but upon his rap for attention they were immediately quiet. However hard the children were worked, they enjoyed their task as Carroll related well to them. Although not given to flattery, he encouraged them. Demanding much from them, he had a clearly defined sense of humour and a keen imagination to which they evidently responded.

In 1926, the choir gave its first public performances – in January at Newton Heath Town Hall, in February at Levenshulme Town Hall, in March at the Free Trade Hall and in October at the Albert Hall. The latter concert was in connection with Civic Week celebrations. The concert on 26 March was the first of the Annual Concerts given by the choir and the Schoolchildren's Orchestra. Carroll reported that on each occasion there was a large and enthusiastic audience.

The number on the register in 1926 was 300; the average weekly attendance was 240. In that period of high unemployment, it was difficult to retain boys in the choir, for they frequently took paid

Manchester's music adviser

jobs after school hours. The teachers in the schools sent promising pupils to Gertrude Riall. Children with evident talent were sent to Carroll's room in Manchester Education Offices, where he further tested them. Strict, fatherly, but kind and patient, he proved to be a lasting example and means of encouragement to many of these schoolchildren.

Key singers were kept in the choir for about four years. At the age of eleven, selection for grammar schools took place. Grammar school pupils were not allowed to sing in the choir; they had, in any case, their own choirs and orchestras. Choristers left at the age of fourteen, or, if they were pupils at central schools, at the age of fifteen. About fifty pupils left during each session because they were unwilling to keep up to Carroll's high standards, or because they were expelled. Hence, at the commencement of each session, a new choir was formed.

In 1928, Carroll reported that the choir worked with great vigour but not a few difficulties:

"It is not easy to keep together, after school hours, a body of 250 boys and girls drawn from all parts of the city. Difficulties abound. Dark winter nights, bad weather and illness are but a few of the obstacles which have to be surmounted. For four seasons, however, the choir has emerged victorious and succeeded, against all odds, in completing its programme." (15)

1928 was a particularly important year for Carroll and the choir: the Third Annual Concert, which took place on 26 March, proved to be an event whose results could hardly have been predicted by Carroll or any one of his young singers. The audience included Hamilton Harty, whom Carroll had invited to attend. Harty was so impressed by the skills and freshness of the young singers that he expressed the wish that they should sing, accompanied by the Hallé Orchestra, at one of the Municipal Concerts during the following winter season. Carroll's work, and that of Gertrude Riall and his other assistants, could hardly have received a greater accolade.

When the concert was being arranged, Harty wrote to Carroll

Manchester's music adviser

from his home in County Down: "The children's music for 4 March, 1929 is excellent and should make a very interesting programme."

On 4 March, 1929, the Manchester Elementary Schools' Choir, accompanied by one of Europe's renowned orchestras, conducted by Hamilton Harty, sang at the final concert of the season's Municipal Concerts. In a characteristic tribute to his young singers, Carroll wrote: "In technique, and still more in spirit, the work of the choir was a revelation of the high services to the art, and to the public, which the children of our schools are capable of rendering." (16)

Accompanied by the Hallé Orchestra, the choir sang eleven pieces, all from memory:

Bach,	*My heart, ever faithful.*
Handel,	*Let the bright seraphim.*
Purcell,	*Nymphs and Shepherds.*
Brahms,	*6 Gypsy Songs*, orchestrated by Eric Fogg.
Humperdinck,	"There stands a little man" "Brother, come and dance" } (*Hansel and Gretel*).

Harty invited the children to make a gramophone recording with the Hallé Orchestra. This recording of an Elementary Schools' Choir and a professional symphony orchestra – unique in British music education – took place on 4 June, 1929. Over fifty years later, it remains a classic in the history of gramophone recordings. Two songs with orchestral accompaniments were placed permanently on record – *Nymphs and Shepherds* by Purcell, and the Dance Duet from the opera *Hansel and Gretel* by Humperdinck. The Columbia Gramophone Company recorded the performers in the Free Trade Hall. The recording, Columbia 9909, a 12-inch 78r.p.m. double-sided disc, "went straight to the hearts of millions of people all over the world". (17) It sold over one million copies, and was re-issued on the Columbia disc, *Angelic Voices*. The Purcell song also appears on the E.M.I. Starline disc, *The Golden Classics*.

A tribute to the choir's achievement appeared in an editorial in *The Music Teacher*:

Manchester's music adviser

"Musicians, aware that Doctor Carroll has held the office of musical adviser to the Manchester Education Committee for several years, will not need to be told why Manchester has a model scheme. Any who care to know something of the scheme in action need only buy Columbia record number 9909, and they will hear the Manchester Elementary Schools' Choir singing with the Hallé Orchestra. They will admit that only a really sound scheme could produce a symptom of that kind . . . here is a delightful choir of happy children." (18)

250 children (160 boys and 90 girls) took part in the recording session. Held in the morning, the first 'take' did not achieve the required standard; the children were dull, unresponsive, unsmiling and evidently overawed by the occasion. The second 'take' was also poor. At this point Gertrude Riall rose and firmly reproached the children. The third 'take' was satisfactory, although by now the children were tired. Carroll and Harty were delighted with the results.

Entirely free from forced tone, and revealing a marvellous flexibility across the whole range, the choir has a rhythmic vitality, secure intonation, sense of musical line and phrasing, and a delightful buoyant tone that can only be described as legendary. The slight tendency to hurry in the opening of the Humperdinck duet underlines the live quality of the sound, the sense of excitement of the actual occasion for these children, and emphasises Harty's skill in maintaining the ensemble.

A member of the choir, present during the recording, testified to the children who took part as "children of the depression", many of whom at home ate "bread and dripping" and "Lancashire hot-pot without meat". The recording and concert performances with the Hallé Orchestra represented a "highlight of our lives". The children were "transformed on stage". (19)

Fifty years later, on the evening of 18 June, 1975, the Golden Jubilee of the Inaugural Concert of the Manchester Elementary Schools' Choir and the Forty-sixth Anniversary of the recording

Manchester's music adviser

were honoured at a Civic Reception in the Manchester Town Hall by the Lord Mayor, Dame Kathleen Ollerenshaw, and Council of the City of Manchester. Honoured guests were Gertrude Riall (Mrs. T. R. Bromley), Edna Jamieson (Mrs. E. Hall), and Elsa and Ida Carroll.

Most of the former members, including at least twenty from the original choir of 1925, came from Greater Manchester. Others came from Jersey, the west of England, Scotland, Wales, Australia and the United States of America. Altogether 220 of the original 250 singers attended a remarkable reunion. The reunion organiser, Stanley Rose, said, "Nostalgia is bringing them back. You must remember that this was a remarkable experience for Manchester school-children – to go on the same platform with Harty and the Hallé. We have never forgotten it." (20) Among the guests was Harold Jones, sub-leader of the Hallé Orchestra in 1929. He expressed the view of the members of the orchestra at the recording session: "It was a most thrilling experience to hear those young, eager and sincere voices singing so brilliantly – it was something never to be forgotten." (21)

The link across fifty years and several continents brings Carroll's own words into perspective:

"Boys and girls, if properly taught, realise that they are learning something which will give them a link with mankind as a whole; a means of social contact even in a strange land." (22)

As a sequel to their fine singing in 1929, the choir were invited to sing at the Municipal Concert on 17 March, 1930. On this occasion the selected choral works included music from *Midsummer Night's Dream* by Mendelssohn.

Carroll established a Children's Music Fund with the surplus money remaining after the success of the Annual Concerts given by the Manchester schoolchildren in the Free Trade Hall. The Fund, assisted by additional donations, was administered to assist children of musical talent whose parents did not possess the means of purchasing and repairing musical instruments. In 1929, the

Manchester's music adviser

Manchester City Council decided that the profits from the Columbia recording should be divided equally between deprived children and the Hallé Orchestra.

At the Municipal Concert held on 9 March, 1931, the Schoolchildren's Choir, for the third year in succession, appeared, accompanied by the Hallé Orchestra. They performed sixteen pieces, all from memory, prepared in twenty-four rehearsals, of one hour each, after school hours:

 Bach,   *Praise God.*
 Bach,   *Of Flowers the Fairest.*
 Humperdinck, "Sleep Fairy's Song" ⎫
        "Prayer"   ⎬ (*Hansel and Gretel*).
 Brahms, *6 Gypsy Songs.*
6 Folk Songs of the British Isles.

The children's average age was $12\frac{1}{2}$ years; they had no previous knowledge of the music. As a result of this performance, the choir were invited to make a radio broadcast from the Manchester Broadcasting Station. The Station Director, in a letter of appreciation, enclosed a contribution of five guineas to the Children's Music Fund. Further wireless broadcasts took place in April 1932, April 1933, and May 1934.

After the success of the Columbia record and the three years (1929–1931) when the choir sang with the Hallé Orchestra, Carroll and Harty planned to take the choir to give concerts in Hamburg. However, the threatening situation on the Continent prevented it. Harty resigned his Hallé post in 1933 and Carroll retired in the following year. The choir continued its work until the 1939–1945 War, when, although the large body of members no longer met, small groups presented programmes on the radio.

The choir was not re-formed after the War. Its period of greatest success, educational value and concert-giving had been a short one, from 1925 to 1934, but its educational influence on the formative years of hundreds of Manchester schoolchildren was inestimable.

Manchester's music adviser
MUSIC IN INFANTS' SCHOOLS

IN the spring of 1926, a year after the *Handbook of Music* had been issued, Carroll organised a series of five demonstration lectures given in the Onward Hall, to cover the special needs of teachers in infants' schools. Applications for membership having reached a total of 700, the lectures were given in duplicate in order that all could attend.

A further, similar course was organised in 1929, when the number of applicants rose to 776. Carroll stressed the important and exacting role of the infant school teacher of music, suggesting that a great degree of flexibility was necessary for the application of the principles and practical demonstrations at this level, for "so undeveloped is the reasoning faculty of the pupil that the wise teacher is ever ready to swerve aside from the beaten track of academic rule into the fresher byways of imagination and analogy." (23)

In June 1929, the Manchester Education Committee issued a booklet by Carroll entitled *Music in Infants' Schools*. This was a summary of the demonstration lectures given in 1926 and 1929. It appeared, with minor modifications, as the opening section of the 1934 edition of the *Handbook of Music*.

Carroll's dedication to the work of teaching very young children continued up to his retirement. In August 1933, he organised a course of eight lectures for teachers in infant and junior schools, in the Onward Hall:

1. Foundations of Musical Training.
2. The Voice in Speaking and Singing.
3. Aural Work in Modern Teaching.
4. Music in the Child's First Term.
5. Early Lessons in Notation.
6. Songs, Rounds and Partsongs.
7. Hymns and Simple Anthems.
8. Rhythm and Natural Movement.

The first two lectures were illustrated by Carroll; the remainder by classes from schools. Altogether 325 teachers attended this course.

MUSIC IN SECONDARY SCHOOLS

ALTHOUGH Carroll's work as Music Adviser was mainly with the elementary schools of Manchester, his interest and ideas were not confined to the elementary stage. On 26 February, 1930, having completed a period of special supervision over the city's secondary schools, he issued a Memorandum, *Adolescent Boys and Girls: Use of the Voice for Singing*. In this document, Carroll gave support to the view that adolescent boys should refrain entirely from singing. In the case of girls' singing at this stage, he advised that, although the change in a girl's voice was less marked, there should be an avoidance of solo singing lessons, solo competitive work with its mental and physical strains, and choral works containing severe difficulties. Ordinary singing in a girls' choir was, however, highly recommended.

Carroll was careful, in this document, to state that although his opinions were the result of careful research, he did not regard them as final, but subject to modifications. Indeed, in the booklet, *Music in Manchester Schools: 1918–1930*, published in April 1930, Carroll reveals awareness that, because of the singing difficulties and pressure from examination subjects, all music lessons were discontinued at the adolescent period in many boys' secondary schools. He argued that the boys with "broken" voices were still capable of singing or humming in the vital areas of aural culture and sight-singing.

He regretted that the composition of melodies, the study of notation, elementary harmony, studies in rhythm, and musical history employing the gramophone, were absent from the curriculum in the upper forms of many boys' secondary schools. Although musical appreciation, attendance at concerts and discussions on music were encouraged, the musical life of these schools did not compare with the standard of music-making in the girls' secondary schools.

Manchester's music adviser

Carroll argued strongly for an integrated approach to music, movement and drama in his Memorandum, *Qualifications of a Music Mistress or Music Master for a High School, Secondary School or other Institution*. Several pupils showing outstanding gifts in music or dance were granted special facilities in the secondary schools on the submission of Headteachers. In 1930, Carroll noted that fifteen boys and girls possessing unique promise had been found: all received advice or assistance in the development of their particular abilities.

Among the dancers whom Carroll assisted in their early years, was Edna Squire-Brown, later to become Principal Dancer at the Coliseum and Alhambra Theatres in London and originator of the "Dance of the Doves". She maintained correspondence with Carroll into his last years, giving him details of her career and stressing the childhood debt that she owed to him and to Spurley Hey.

MUSIC IN MANCHESTER SCHOOLS: 1918–1930

THIS booklet, written by Carroll, reviewed the twelve years' progress in music education in the city's schools from the time of his part-time trial appointment until four years before his retirement. In the Preface, Spurley Hey paid tribute to Carroll's work:

"The period from 1918 to 1930 has seen the establishment of the teaching of Music in the Elementary Schools of Manchester as a fundamental subject of the curriculum. The Committee were extremely fortunate in the appointment of Dr. Walter Carroll as Musical Adviser, and Dr. Carroll has been equally fortunate in the members of his special staff, in the excellent attitude of the teachers towards the development of Music in their schools, and in the splendid response of the children to its influence."

Spurley Hey wrote this Preface a few days before his fatal illness. Carroll was always conscious of the debt which he, the Manchester teachers and children owed to the support and far-sighted policies of the Director of Education. They were, in fact, close friends as well as

Manchester's music adviser

colleagues, and could often be seen walking together in the mornings along Deansgate to the Education Offices – the huge, bulky figure of Hey and the slight frame of Carroll at his side. Hey died of pneumonia on 7 May, 1930, after just four days' illness. Carroll was deeply shocked. Shortly afterwards he expressed his gratitude for Hey's Preface to his booklet:

"It was the last of a long series of wise suggestions and generous actions which, from time to time, had stimulated the progress and spirit of the work.

The Musical Adviser desires to place on record his deep sense of gratitude for all the valuable help and encouragement which he received from his late Chief." (24)

Reviewing Carroll's booklet and his work in music education for the children of Manchester, a correspondent of *The Times Educational Supplement* wrote:

"none has undertaken the task more thoroughly, nor have the results been generally available in such completeness or in so clear a form . . . The Manchester line of development from a power to perform well and a power to hear well to the culminating power to utilize well is a lesson on which all committees could model any development." (25)

FINAL YEARS AS MUSIC ADVISER

AT the Lancashire Education Committee Conference for Head Teachers of Junior Evening Institutes, held at St. Annes-on-Sea in May 1930, Carroll, in advocating a case for a more liberal curriculum, advised that courses in the appreciation of music ought to be commenced in well-populated districts where there was a progressive, well-known school which could be utilised as a centre. He recommended one or two classes, each of an hour's length, to be held each week, open to students and citizens in general: a far-sighted move to what in more recent times has been called "community schooling".

Manchester's music adviser

By this date, 400 schools in Manchester were working under his musical direction. There were also twenty-eight Junior Evening Institutes; twenty of these had singing classes. Carroll now had a staff of six: Emily Allen, Dr. Stanley Grundy, Dr. Christie Green, Rose Evans, Gertrude Riall and (a new appointment in 1928) Dr. Dennis Chapman.

In 1934, having reached the compulsory retirement age of 65, Carroll relinquished his post as Music Adviser to Manchester Education Committee. The last of his Reports concludes with a farewell note:

"EPILOGUE"

"In presenting this, the last of his Annual Reports, the Musical Adviser ventures to touch a personal note before giving, in conclusion, a progressive outline of the work accomplished in Manchester during the past sixteen years. To the Education Committee he is deeply grateful for the large measure of freedom and confidence which he has been privileged to enjoy throughout his term of office, and for many other tokens of interest and appreciation. From the late Director, Mr. Spurley Hey, he received help and encouragement of unique value in the creation of what was then a new Department. It was due to this wide guidance and breadth of outlook that the benefits of Music Appreciation were brought into touch with the poorer parts of the city. Under the watchful interest and cordial support of the present Director progress has been well sustained. To him, to many other officers of the Committee, and especially to the members of the Music Staff, the Musical Adviser offers his sincere thanks. He assures them that their attitude of kindness and consideration has greatly enhanced the fruitfulness of his labours.

Every ending has in it a tinge of sadness. Work which is really loved can be the finest of all recreation, and the closing of a long and happy trust may well resemble the passing of a valued friend. But in the field of Education no task is ever finished, and the present change is but an opportunity for further advance. The teachers and the scholars have responded well. They will respond again. They

Manchester's music adviser

hold firmly the conviction that the musical training provided for the children will continue, unbroken and unimpaired, and that the Manchester Education Committee will, in the future as in the past, be regarded as leader in the domain of musical education."

Since his appointment in 1918, Carroll had given about 1200 specimen lessons in elementary schools and about 200 evening lectures demonstrating the Manchester scheme of music education in towns ranging from Spennymoor in the north, to London in the south-east and Bristol in the west of England. 11,187 Manchester schoolteachers had attended his twenty-nine courses of 232 lectures. At the time of his retirement, 12,000 children were included in the scheme for teaching musical appreciation.

Throughout his eighteen years as Music Adviser, he had striven to put into practice principles, methods and techniques founded upon a deep consideration of the values of music in schools. These values had been clearly stated by Carroll in November 1921, to an audience of educationists at Wigan:

1. The value of music for its own sake.
2. The mental value of well-taught music.
3. The value of self-expression as a preparation for leisure.
4. The social value.
5. The spiritual value, appealing to the spirit by the emotions and imagination.

Notwithstanding the essential support, financial, material and professional, necessary for the furtherance of his beliefs and ideals during the following years, it was Carroll's personality that spearheaded the progressive attitude to music education:

"The driving force, however, behind all the musical activity of the Education Committee is his own infinite capacity for taking pains. By no means large in stature, he is nevertheless a giant in accomplishment." (26)

A letter from the Headmaster of the Central School, Newton Heath, Manchester, summed up the experience of a long-serving teacher who had witnessed the development of "singing" to "music" in schools, the broadening of the music curriculum, and the influence of Carroll:

"22 August, 1939

... those of us who were privileged to be Headmasters before you became Musical Adviser to the Education Committee know what a revolution you made in the teaching of music in the schools ...

John H. Kay"

National developments in school music, a willingness to question generally accepted views and the official position, to test theories, to fight for the rights of poorer children, to encourage the gifted in music, to urge a progressive attitude – all these were achieved largely owing to the work of Walter Carroll in Manchester.

chapter six

Matthay School

Music Teachers' Association. Hilda Collens. Holiday Courses. Carroll as honorary lecturer.

IN 1909, Carroll was elected President of the Music Teachers' Association in Manchester. During the session 1909 to 1910, a lecture on the appreciation of music was given by Tobias Matthay. Present at the lecture was a member of the Association, Hilda Collens. Born in 1883, she taught at Sale High School for Girls.

Hilda Collens was greatly impressed by Matthay's work in the field of piano teaching. Whilst Matthay was an inspiration to her, Carroll was an immediate source of practical advice. She came under the influence of his energetic personality and progressive ideas at meetings and became a regular visitor to Carroll's home.

In 1914, Hilda Collens took over the teaching of the Matthay piano students in Manchester. Dynamic, devoted to teaching and in sympathy with the work and ideals of Matthay, Carroll and Stewart Macpherson, she set about broadening the training of her Matthay pupils. In spite of his busy life, Carroll offered support and encouragement in her ideas.

On 20 September, 1920, Hilda Collens established her own music school with nine girls as students, in a small studio above Hime and Addison's music shop in Deansgate. It became known as the Matthay School of Music, Manchester. The school grew with an

Matthay School

extending range of courses emphasising the development of musicianship, musical appreciation, and improved standards of teaching.

Carroll proved to be a powerful ally in the establishment of her Matthay School. By 1923, it had a training course for teachers. In the same year, Gertrude Riall commenced work as a teacher of singing at the school, and trained the choir with the same skill and enthusiasm that she showed with the Schoolchildren's Choir. In 1924, on Carroll's advice, the Manchester Education Committee Music Scholarship was awarded to a young pianist, Irene Wilde, who began studies at the Matthay School. She was the first holder of this award to study there. It appears that Carroll, whose name had been so closely bound up with the Royal Manchester College of Music since its foundation in 1893, was criticised by many who felt that the Music Scholarship holders ought to study at the Royal College instead of the newer, private music school. Impressed, however, by Hilda Collens and her work at the new School, he considered that, with its emphasis on the training of teachers and its friendly atmosphere, it would prove a fine institution for promising musicians.

Carroll's views on the Matthay School, Manchester, were held with conviction and firmness. On his advice, Music Scholarships were awarded by Manchester Education Committee to a further nine pupils for study there. Carroll sent his own daughter, Ida, a fine pianist and double bass player, to the Matthay School in 1922.

After his retirement in 1934, Carroll's influence on the Matthay School grew considerably. On 8 December, 1936, he was Chairman of the Distribution of Awards at the Milton Hall, Manchester. At the reunion dinner on 8 January, 1937, he was nominated, together with Macpherson, a Vice-President of the Matthay School Old Students' Association. One result of the formation of this association was the publication of a School Magazine in July 1937. Carroll wrote a short article, *Success*, for the first issue.

In 1937, Carroll gave the first of the summer lectures given by distinguished visitors to the Matthay School. He spoke about a

Matthay School

recent week he had spent on a lecture tour in South Wales where his audience included unemployed miners. He contrasted the desperate poverty of the depressed areas with the unbroken spirit of the men and their devotion to music. The study and appreciation of music was to these men, as it was to Carroll, more than a hobby or pastime: it was an essential and ennobling feature of life.

From 1937, Carroll lectured on many occasions and chaired the Distribution of Awards several times at the Matthay School. A notable event of 1939 at the School was a series of twenty lectures given by Carroll on *Principles and Methods of Teaching applied to Music*. He demonstrated his arguments with a class of boys. It was noted that "Dr. Carroll seems to have an uncanny knack of understanding the working of the child mind and the best ways in which to appeal to it." (1) On 1 August, he lectured on *The Magic of Mind and Music* and *Songs for Young Singers*. During the latter lecture, dealing with the training of the voice, he used ten small boys to provide music examples. It was reported that "Dr. Carroll is at his best with boys; his benevolent amusement at their mistakes never irritates them; his fund of humorous anecdotes diverts them, and his constant encouragement spurs them to further efforts." (2) Aged 70, he had lost neither skills nor charisma.

Carroll's energy and enthusiasm for the cause of music education continued throughout the war years. On 19 July, 1940, he lectured on *How Composers Compose* at the Holiday Course for Teachers. During the autumn term, he gave a course of ten lectures on *The Anatomy of Music*. He organised a series of concerts for the armed forces in the spring of 1941, held every two weeks on Sunday evenings at the Young Men's Christian Association in Manchester; Matthay School students provided the items. In the same year he was appointed Honorary Musical Adviser to the School. From January to April 1941, he gave ten lectures at the School on *The Art of Teaching*. In the autumn he gave a further ten lectures on *Character Training*, a course which he repeated in the early autumn of 1942.

In her Report of 1942, Hilda Collens expressed the School's debt

Matthay School

to Carroll:

"Dr. Carroll himself has been an equally staunch friend and since my earliest teaching days his help and influence have been a wonderful inspiration. Neither Mr. Macpherson nor Dr. Carroll ever had any financial connection with the School, a fact which has made their friendship all the more outstanding." (3)

In 1941, the Matthay School had been in existence for twenty-one years. It now had premises in Oxford Road, Manchester, close to the University and the Royal Manchester College of Music. The staff totalled 30 and there were nearly 200 students. Hilda Collens decided that it was essential to alter the School from a private to a public institution. In the autumn of 1943, it became known as "The Northern School of Music". At the first meeting of the Council, on 2 November, 1943, a company secretary was appointed – Ida Carroll.

In his mid-seventies Carroll retained his skills as a lecturer, for in 1944 he gave two lectures, illustrated by students of the Northern School of Music, in Stretford, Manchester. The first of these lectures was given to elementary schoolchildren, the second to members of various youth organisations. A request for a further two similar lectures reveals evidence of his success.

The Annual Distribution of Awards on 6 March, 1945, was marked by Carroll's absence for the first time. He chaired no more meetings at the Northern School of Music, although he remained a Vice-President until his death. On the thirtieth anniversary of the School, an Editorial in the Magazine referred to Carroll as "a familiar and dearly-loved Manchester figure". (4) Hilda Collens wrote of him as one "who helped in more ways than could be mentioned." (5)

chapter seven

Sacred music

Choirmaster and director of music at St. James's Church, Birch, Manchester. Sacred compositions.

ST. JAMES'S Parish Church, Birch-in-Rusholme, Manchester, consecrated on 1 July, 1846, by the Bishop of Chester, and built in the early English Gothic style, still retained the atmosphere of a rural establishment within an industrial city in the early decades of the twentieth century. In 1916, its Director of Music joined the armed forces. Carroll agreed to take over the post of Honorary Choirmaster and Director of Music for a short period. In fact he remained until 1938, completing twenty-two years of service.

During his years at St. James's Church, Carroll also organised many concerts, frequently incorporating explanatory and illustrative material, in the manner of his lectures and talks on musical appreciation to schools and teachers.

Carroll had first come under the influence of the great Anglican choral tradition when he was aged seventeen. He had not served the church as a choirboy; he disliked the "hooty" tone produced by many Anglican choirs. Instead he preferred the natural beauty of fresh young voices with, in mixed choirs, boys and girls intermingled in soprano and alto parts.

His fine anthem, *Sleep Thy Last Sleep*, written in 1923, to words by E. A. Dayman for the Commemoration of the Armistice, is characterised by smooth part-writing, expressive harmony and imaginative word-painting:

(i).

(ii).

Carroll saw his vocation as educator and musician in a wider context than the confines of the school classroom, however important that might be. His work as organist and choirmaster was, for him, a truly educative mission. He took a leading position in the National Union of Organists, being unanimously elected President of the Manchester Association on 10 May, 1919, and served as delegate and committee member to the National Union of Organists' Associations. From 1904 to 1949, he was a member of the

Sacred music

Royal College of Organists.

He lectured regularly to organists' associations, including, apart from towns in the Manchester area, Blackburn, Edinburgh, Nottingham, Preston and Southport. His reputation in the wider field of music education was known and held in high regard by the various organists' associations. It was asserted:

"During the past five years there has been much progress in the musical instruction of young people throughout the country, and tribute might be paid to such men as Dr. Walter Carroll and others who are doing so much in the direction of presenting music in such form as to make the young mind thoroughly appreciative." (1)

At the Annual Congress of Delegates of the National Union of Organists held in Manchester on 1 September, 1926, Carroll lectured on *The Training of a Voluntary Choir*. In this lecture he stated that:

"The aim, unassailable in its truth and simplicity, is Service to God . . . The true choirmaster is an artist and as such is completely absorbed in his work. He *serves* his work; in so doing he serves God and he serves his fellow-men." (2)

In this lecture he discussed in detail the recruiting and composition of choirs, general organisation and rehearsals, and the conduct of the Divine Service. In particular, he revealed his understanding and affection for the choirboy:

"the least permanent but the most vital element, the keystone of the musical arch, is the boy chorister . . . There is something unexpected about the choirboy. He is like a streak of light in a dark place. The supreme cause of unrest, he is also the supreme cure for dullness. He is as lovable as he is tiresome. The whole stability of the choir depends upon the boys, and the choirmaster is wise who makes their training his first care." (3)

On the occasion of Carroll's retirement from St. James's Church, the Rector wrote:

"Dr. Carroll is first and foremost a teacher of music, and in his

Sacred music

long service at Birch he freely consecrated his gift to the Divine Service. Of his meticulous care, of his unfailing regularity, of his painstaking perseverance, and of his scrupulous regard for his office, how can I write? Are not these things written in the chronicles of Birch and in the memory of its clergy and people?"

Carroll's principal compositions for church choir belong, however, not to his Birch years, but to 1902 and 1903. Fluent in ideas and skilled craftsmanship, their eclecticism evokes echoes of Schubert, Mendelssohn and the sacred style of Sullivan, as in the *Magnificat and Nunc Dimittis in F* dating from 1902:

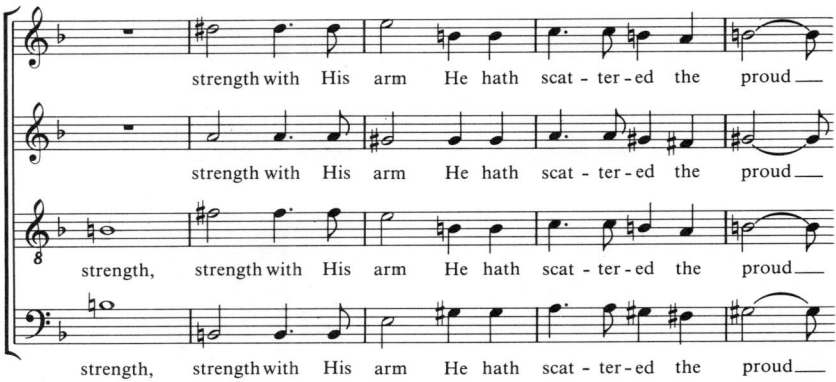

1903 saw the publication of *Te Deum Laudamus* and *Jubilate Deo*,

Sacred music

both in F major. The first of these two choral works reveals dramatic contrasts of tempo and dynamics and vivid word-painting:

Jubilate Deo opens with vigorous vocal lines in characteristic English manner:

Sacred music

In contrast to these extended choral pieces, there was published at the same time a short *Vesper Hymn*:

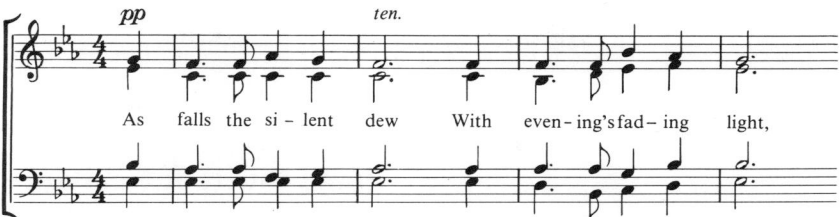

In producing these choral works which he later taught to his choir at St. James's Church, Carroll was following the fashion of Victorian and Edwardian composers in England, who in writing for amateur choirs chose the subjects they preferred above all others – religious themes.

Carroll's choral music, like so much of this genre from Victorian and Edwardian times, is now rarely performed. Just as Sullivan, writer of largely forgotten oratorios and cantatas, is remembered for his sparkling comic operas, so Carroll lives on in his music for children.

chapter eight

Piano music for children

Carroll's piano teaching editions. Carroll's original piano compositions for children: a new age in the musical education of children.

BY the close of the nineteenth century, the upright piano, a status symbol of great significance, was appearing frequently in working-class homes in England. Referring to the material possessions sought after by poor families in the Manchester and Salford areas prior to the First World War, Robert Roberts, author of *The Classic Slum*, wrote that "luxury articles most longed for were pianos." (1) Children in industrial cities frequently travelled to the pleasanter suburbs for piano lessons.

In the later years of the nineteenth century and the early years of the twentieth century, an analytical approach was brought to the subject of piano-teaching, part of the general movements in investigation and broadening of music education. Carroll openly acknowledged his support for the principles and methods put forward by Tobias Matthay and Mrs. Annie Curwen.

Carroll's first publication was two Sonatinas for piano, in C major and D major, published in 1892 by Forsyth Brothers. He evidently intended these three-movement works for the use of players of limited ability, for they were re-published in 1914 as *Six Easy Studies in the Olden Style*. Revealing the influence of the sonatinas of Clementi and the fingerwork characteristic of Weber,

Piano music for children

they can serve as preparatory material for the study of the easier movements of Mozart's sonatas:

(i). From Study number 2:

(ii). From Study number 3:

CARROLL'S PIANO TEACHING EDITIONS

THE late nineteenth and early twentieth centuries saw much activity in the editing of earlier keyboard music. Carroll, trained in the academic practice of Baroque techniques, edited and fingered performing editions of pieces by Bach, Corelli, Handel and Kirnberger from 1908 to 1912. These editions, expressly produced for teaching purposes, were all published by Forsyth.

Carroll's first publication for young pianists was a graded selection of sixteen short pieces mostly from J. S. Bach's

Piano music for children

Clavierbüchlein for Anna Magdalena Bach. The collection, *First Lessons in Bach*, Book 1, was published in 1908. Carroll's object in producing this edition of eight Minuets, three Marches, two Musettes, one Bourrée, one Gavotte and one Polonaise was the provision of unsimplified, easy teaching pieces by a major composer, in a clear performing text.

Carroll wrote a short preface to the collection and included dynamics, fingering and phrase-marks for the guidance of teacher and pupil. At the start of each piece he put an Italian tempo indication, a suggested metronome marking and a sentence pointing to the special technical or interpretative aspects.

The period when this collection was published witnessed a growing appreciation of the music of Bach. Carroll wrote:

"The performance of his incomparable works, whose influence flows in an ever widening channel through the whole domain of musical education, has clearly demonstrated that the practical study of Bach is the gateway to the mastery of technique." (2)

Further, he viewed these pieces from a dual standpoint – both as studies in elementary technical details and as pieces of charm and refinement. Highly successful as an edition of short and simple pieces for children, they played an important role in the wider appreciation of the music of Bach.

In 1909, a further volume was published: *First Lessons in Bach*, Book 2. This collection of twelve short pieces, rather more difficult than those in Book 1, contains three Minuets, three Gavottes, three Polonaises, one Prelude, one Sarabande and one Scherzo from varied sources, including the *Clavierbüchlein*. As in the earlier volume, the pieces are graded, fingered and phrased, with hints on the main technical or interpretative features. This volume was intended to serve as a link between the first book and the Little Preludes or the Two-part Inventions of J. S. Bach. In his Preface Carroll wrote:

"The remarkable success which has attended the publication of *First Lessons in Bach*, and the wide measure of approval accorded to it by music teachers in all parts of the country, have encouraged the compiler to issue a second book of short pieces . . . the first set has conclusively proved that Bach can be taught successfully, and learnt with enjoyment, in the elementary course."

In 1910, Carroll made a piano arrangement of the Gigue from Corelli's Sonata in A for violin and continuo. This was published as the first number in a new series, Forsyth's Classical Library. 1911 and 1912 saw the publication of the next two numbers in the series – both edited and fingered by Carroll – the Allegro from Handel's Harpsichord Suite in G minor and a two-part Fugue in D by Kirnberger. The latter was his final example of editing, for in the same year he commenced his series of original teaching pieces for children.

CARROLL'S ORIGINAL PIANO COMPOSITIONS FOR CHILDREN

FIRST PIANO LESSONS BOOK ONE: SCENES AT A FARM (1912)

AT this period of his life, Carroll was exceedingly busy, committed to his Professorship at the Royal Manchester College of Music, lecturing at the University, and membership of academic and professional bodies. At the same time he was formulating, developing and testing his theories on the art of teaching and the teaching of music to young children.

On her fourth birthday, he gave his daughter, Ida, her first piano lesson. Her weekly lessons occupied about ten minutes, divided roughly as follows:

Playing a familiar work	– 3 minutes.
Learning a new work	– 3 minutes.
Duet playing	– 2 minutes.
Marching and clapping whilst the teacher plays	– 2 minutes. (3)

To Ida, her father's attitude was kind but strict, with special attention being given to accuracy, fingering, phrasing, nuance and

Piano music for children

quality of tone. These earliest piano lessons were supported by much work on the training of the ear, sol-fa and general musicianship. Neither father nor daughter possessed perfect pitch, but a very good sense of relative pitch. Ida used to practise the piano after school, in her father's study, when he was not using it.

Dissatisfied with the teaching material available for piano teachers of the very young, Carroll decided to write his own short pieces for children. A definite stimulus came from a family holiday spent, in the summer of 1911, in the small fishing village of Portpatrick in south-west Scotland. On returning home to Manchester, Walter and Ida, filled with memories of the natural beauty of fields and woods, sea and countryside, found that "the Tutor, with its grim cover and queer contents, seemed very dull." (4) Carroll composed, for his daughter's lessons, some short, imaginative pieces centred around a farmhouse which they had visited whilst staying at Portpatrick. Quite unlike the books of scales and finger exercises, and the tutors with their highly technical and austere methods, these short pieces, with their descriptive titles, were transcribed into a small manuscript book dated 11 February, 1912. In later years he said that this was the hardest piece of composing he had ever attempted. The result of his labours was a small miracle.

When *Scenes at a Farm* was published in 1912, it helped to establish a new approach to the teaching of the piano to young children. Believing that finger exercises, tutors and instruction books, advocated by untrained teachers, had caused much stiff and clumsy playing among average pianists, partly because of the problems of attempting to control the finger and hand muscles whilst at the same time concentrating the mind on the printed notes, Carroll wrote that "in technique looseness should come before control, and control before strength. The early practice of finger exercises from a printed copy is detrimental to both qualities, especially the former." (5)

Carroll recommended that at about the age of six, after much preparatory work in singing and sight-reading, practice in melody, rhythm and games, action songs, the development of aural

Piano music for children

perception, and listening to music, the pupil should be given about ten short lessons in time and pitch. This work, building on the pupil's previous musical experiences, laying the foundations of musicianship and literacy, was to precede the actual technique of preliminary stages at the piano. Carroll referred teachers to his booklet published in 1912, *Notes on the Teaching of First Piano Lessons,* for the content of these early lessons in notation. These ten lessons formed part of his course of lectures in the Art of Teaching at the Royal Manchester College of Music.

If the pupil had some knowledge of the staff, the piano pieces could be started immediately; no special physical preparatory work is required. Carroll recommended that the necessary condition of natural looseness could be tested at the instrument by some preliminary exercises shown by the teacher, consisting of single notes or simple chords played by the child, anywhere on the keyboard, using arm weight alone.

Scenes at a Farm, dedicated to his daughters, consists of sixteen short pieces, the last four being duets. In accord with his intention of training the child's imagination, Carroll asked a Cheshire schoolmaster, H. Lang Jones, to write a descriptive verse for each piece. Working from the title of each piece and a copy of the music, H. Lang Jones produced descriptive verses which, based on the rhythmic structure of each piece, could be sung or spoken by the pupil. This integration of the arts, together with the emphasis on the beauty of Nature can be traced to Carroll's absorption of the educational ideals of Froebel, the kindergarten system and Schumann's *Album for the Young.*

1. "The Farmhouse." C major. The right hand plays in 3rds. throughout; the left hand plays a line of single notes, employing C, D and G only. Looseness of arm movement and independence of movement between the arms are among the aims. The verse and piece are quoted in full:

"Down there in the valley, look!
Close beside the winding brook,
Sheltered warm

Piano music for children

From the storm
What a pretty farmhouse!"

2. "The Jolly Farmer." G major. The right hand has a strong melody with an emphasis on the interval of a 5th. Octave doubling is employed for the strong start, underlining the strength and jollity of the farmer:

The intervals of a 2nd., 3rd., 4th. and 5th. appear in the bass, with the thumb acting as a pivotal note:

3. "In the Quiet Wood." G major. A repeated open 5th. (G – D) in the bass supports a quiet right hand chordal part, stressing the interval of a 6th. and introducing the interval of a 2nd. The tie is introduced at the conclusion:

Piano music for children

4. "The Milkmaid's Song." C major. A bright, high-pitched, right-hand melody is supported by a rolling accompaniment of single notes in the left hand. At the end of the piece the semibreve is introduced:

5. "A Morning Ride." C major. A piece with plenty of 10ths. between the hands and 3rds. within each hand:

6. "The Robins." C major. A right-hand melody with a chordal structure has cadence figures utilising a complete dominant 7th. chord in close position:

Piano music for children

7. "On the Lake." C major. A flowing melody mainly in crotchets in the right hand, depicting the gentle gliding of a boat on a lake, is supported by an almost unbroken series of dotted minims in the left hand. Each of the four phrases employs identical opening material:

8. "Girl's Flower Dance." C major. A piece introducing the pupil to imitative technique, with its stress on independence between the two hands:

9. "The Squirrel." G major. The verse begins:

"Up! up! up! up!
Now swinging,
Now springing –"

Carroll's music depicts the squirrel's jumps by loudly accented rising octaves on G. These are contrasted with smooth slurred notes in 3rds.:

The crotchet rest is introduced, in the right hand only.

Piano music for children

10. "The Lost Lamb." A minor. Carroll introduces the pupil to a minor tonality to express the sadness of a lost lamb. As in the second piece, both hands play the melody, one octave apart:

The left hand has now reached two leger lines above the stave.

11. "Going to the Hayfield." C major. Contrasted in mood and tonality to the previous piece, this short 8-bar piece introduces the pupil to staccato touch:

Although the interval of a 4th. had appeared occasionally earlier in the collection, it is a special feature of this piece. The minim rest is introduced in the last bar.

12. "The Cuckoo." F major. Falling staccato 3rds., with the left hand imitating the right hand, are contrasted with legato touch. Crotchet rests are revised, and an anacrusic beginning is introduced for the first time:

Piano music for children

13. "The Little Brook." G major. Consisting of twenty bars, this is the longest piece in the collection so far. Over an ostinato bass, utilising the first and fifth fingers, the right hand plays a melody in 3rds. or 6ths., with an emphasis on octave changes:

The dynamic marking "pp" is introduced for the final chord; the tie is revised.

14. "May-day Dance." G major. This is the longest piece in the collection, consisting of thirty-six bars. Formally, it is in two repeated sections, each consisting of sixteen bars, plus a 4-bar coda. A bright right-hand melody is supported by the left hand playing 3-note chords, using the thumb as a pivot:

15. "Tossing the Hay." C major. A lesson on the same melody at different pitch-levels, incorporating simple imitative technique:

Semibreve and crotchet rests and accent marks are revised.

Piano music for children

16. "Now All Is Sleeping." C major. A fine study in expression, calling on the pupil's imaginative powers to interpret the calm simplicity of the poem:

"The light is dying
 And darkness creeping;
 The birds are flying
 Each to its nest."

Over a repeated 5th. throughout in the bass, the right hand plays subdued two-bar phrases in 2nds., 3rds., 4ths. and 6ths:

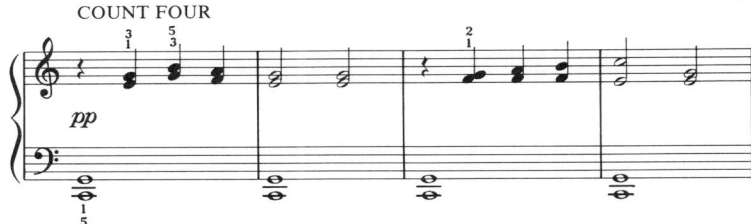

17. Duet: "The March of the Farmer's Men." C major. The second player keeps a steady minim rocking movement, supporting a melody in octaves played by the first player. Carroll advises that the second player can omit the lowest note of the right-hand chords if unable to stretch the complete chord:

Piano music for children

18. Duet: "The Dance of the Shepherd Girls." G major. Staccato crotchets are contrasted with sustained dotted minims in both players' parts. The second player has a simple waltz accompaniment, whilst the first player has a melody in octaves:

19. Duet: "The Lonely Shepherd." A minor. Carroll again chooses a minor key to descibe melancholy. In this short duet, the two players are treated as equals, with weaving, narrow melodic lines:

Piano music for children

20. Duet: "Round the Maypole." C major. A bright and cheerful piece with plenty of staccato touch, chords mostly in 3rds., practice on careful counting of rests, strong accentuation and, in the final two bars, the introduction of "ff" marking and a pause sign. In two repeated sections, the second section opens with the melodic interest passing from the second player to the first player and back again:

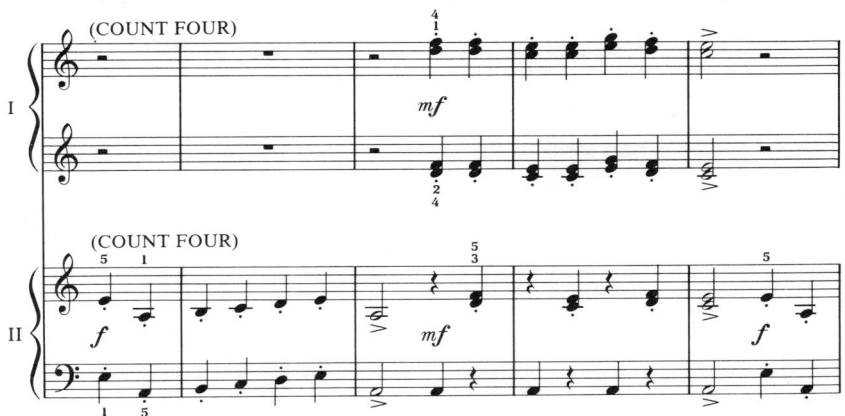

Carroll stressed that even when the pupil had begun to study the pieces from this collection, the teacher should continue with the preliminaries of notation, questioning, illustrating and experimenting to develop the child from within. He laid great emphasis on the importance of ear-training in every lesson: "Recognition of the fact *by ear* must precede or at least accompany, recognition by reasoning and eye." (6)

In order to preserve the natural looseness of the child's fingers, he recommended avoidance of all finger exercises.

The pieces in the collection are varied in key, but without the use of accidentals. The shortest note is the crotchet. Time signatures are not employed, but dynamics and marks of expression appear throughout the volume.

A remarkable feature is the employment of chords, even in the opening piece. Carroll advised teachers to teach their pupils chords of a 3rd., 5th., and even full triads, in the earliest lessons. Many

Piano music for children

simple yet effective passages in this work are built on chords, intending to produce a free arm movement and a greater interest in the pupil than could be achieved by melodic lines alone. He wrote: "Children find thirds delightfully easy to play and are less likely to stiffen than in scale passages." (7)

Carroll believed that in all these pieces the final musical result was not achieved until, having learnt the notes and rhythm correctly, the pupil attempted to portray the title in a sound picture. However inadequate the portrayal might be, it was important that the child should use the imaginative powers. Memory-playing was also to be encouraged. When a pupil had learnt a piece, teachers were advised to play it over with strong accentuation, whilst the pupil walked, marched, or otherwise made rhythmic movements – this was to develop the pupil's perception of time, rhythm, accent and mood.

Pedalling, Carroll recommended, could be used in early study, at the teacher's discretion. The sustaining pedal could be used in the final bars of the first piece; the una corda pedal could be used in number 16: "Now All Is Sleeping" – in both cases to increase the beginner's interest and to vary the tone-colour of the music. He further recommended that children who were interested in drawing and painting ought to be encouraged to produce imaginative reproductions of the scene summoned up by the music.

In his attempt to write teaching pieces for young people, related to their contact with life, integrating several arts in the pursuit of the successful teaching of early piano pupils, Carroll brought to the volume, not only the descriptive verses and titles for each piece, but also a special cover designed by the London artist, Clement Cooke. He was the son of Ebenezer Cooke, who had lectured on singing in 1908 at Carroll's Training Class for Music Teachers.

Carroll was committed to the integration of the arts of music, drawing and poetry in this and his subsequent piano-teaching albums. He looked for fine illustrators to design cover and title pages. The artists were all paid by Carroll himself, at fees ranging from £5 to £50. His decision to incorporate the work of established artists in the illustration of children's music books owed much to the

Piano music for children

support and farsightedness of Forsyth the publishers, to whom he paid tribute in 1951: "to the House of Forsyth for its loyalty, enterprise and understanding". (8)

Scenes at a Farm helped to foster a new, progressive approach to teaching the piano to children. In this, and subsequent volumes, Carroll demonstrated his ability to view early piano lessons from the standpoint of the child, and thus to adopt a style of musical presentation, reasoning and method specially suited to the young mind.

By 1948, 1½ million copies of his children's piano pieces had been sold. Following requests from music teachers in Holland, Carroll and his publishers agreed to the printing of editions in Dutch. Permission was also granted for a production of a braille edition for the National Institute of the Blind.

FIRST PIANO LESSONS BOOK TWO: THE COUNTRYSIDE (1913)

THE success of *Scenes at a Farm* was so marked that, in 1913, a second book of Carroll's teaching pieces was issued, entitled *The Countryside*. This collection, again dedicated to his daughters, contains sixteen solo pieces and two duets, varying in length from eight bars to a full page. Intended to follow *Scenes at a Farm*, or to be used independently, it is a slightly harder collection.

In the first edition, Carroll again simplified the notation, omitting key signatures and putting in accidentals as required but, because he received many letters asking for key signatures to be retained, a second edition was produced to that effect.

The keys employed include those with not more than one sharp or one flat. Time signatures and directions in English appear at the start of each piece. As in the earlier collection, each piece has a title; there are, however, no verses.

During the course of this collection, with its appeal to the imagination, Carroll introduces the child to many aspects of piano technique. The following two contrasted examples reveal how

Piano music for children

Carroll's indications in English at the start of a piece were intended to arouse a precise and imaginative response:

6. "The Rainbow."

13. "Purple Heather."

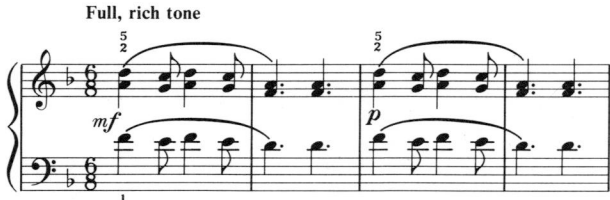

The effect of the directions listed above, together with others such as "With Pity", "Quick and Light", and "With Firm Step", can be underestimated. A similar attempt to appeal directly to the pupil, using simple and evocative phrases was made later in the twentieth century by Benjamin Britten.

Much emphasis is laid on the playing of 3rds. and 6ths. For example, from the opening of number 16, "Lullaby":

Number 14, "The Village Band", provides training in the playing of chords in both hands together:

Piano music for children

Independence of the hands, early steps in part-playing, and the execution of contrasting dynamics figure high in the technical and interpretative skills which this volume aims to develop in the young pianist. Number 4, "Raindrops", is an example of these aspects:

In his Preface to *The Countryside*, Carroll advises that the teacher should question the pupil about the scenes suggested by the titles, in order to stimulate the pupil's imagination. Older pupils could write a short essay about each piece, and possibly construct a story about the whole collection when the volume was finished.

He disliked the cover on the first edition; for the second edition he engaged William Heath Robinson, cartoonist and book-illustrator, to design a new cover. Following correspondence with Carroll, in which he revealed delight at being asked, Heath Robinson produced one of his finest portraits of children and nature, an inspired appeal to the young child's imagination and an essential part of Carroll's attempt to co-ordinate the arts in support of his teaching principles.

SEA IDYLLS (1914)

THE year after the publication of *The Countryside* saw the issuing of ten short pieces to assist pupils in tone-colour and expressive playing

Piano music for children

under the title *Sea Idylls*. The pieces all have descriptive titles.

Carroll described these pieces as "sound-pictures in miniature, suggested by recollections of a visit to the beautiful rockbound shores of Galloway, where the mystery of the sea and the fire of the sunset weave their magic spell around a coast-line full of romantic interest". (9)

Considerably more difficult than the volumes of 1912 and 1913, these pieces have tempo indications in English and metronome markings. Detailed pedalling indications are provided. The pieces cover a wide variety of expressive moods and techniques. Their reliance on simple, attractive melodies, with the support of late-Romantic harmonic structures, provide the pupil with a worthwhile introduction to the *Lyric Pieces* of Grieg and the *Woodland Sketches* and *Forgotten Fairytales* of MacDowell. The following three examples show the varied technical and expressive demands required of the pupil:

Number 6 – "Moonbeams."

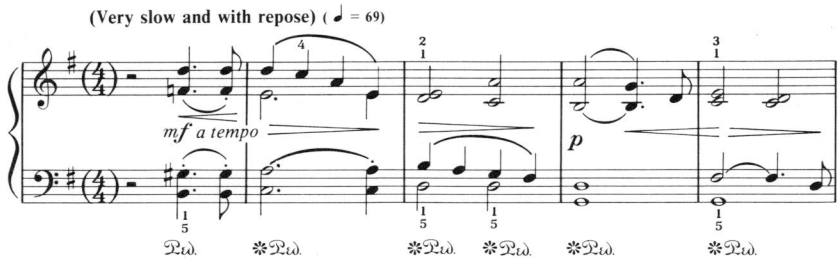

Number 7 – "A Passing Storm."

Piano music for children

Number 8 – "To a Sea Bird."

Intended for pupils of any age, each piece in *Sea Idylls* is prefaced by two lines from the works of varied poets, to stimulate the imagination and create a sense of beauty. Number 6, "Moonbeams", has two lines from Robert Browning:

"The grey sea and the long black land;
And the yellow halfmoon large and low."

Coleridge, Shakespeare and Shelley feature among the poets Carroll chose for the other pieces.

Sea Idylls was also intended as a course of memory-training for pupils. Carroll held strong views on the benefits of memory-playing, stating:

"Something *must* be done each week without the copy, if it be but four bars ... *Every* child can play from memory; it may not be much but it can be something every week, and a something which grows and grows until at the age of ten a whole movement seems quite easy to remember." (10)

He declared that the pupil whose memory had been trained always played when asked, and usually performed with greater precision and confidence than the child who was totally reliant on the printed copy. This progressive view was not shared by many piano teachers early in the twentieth century, who tended to discourage playing from memory because, they argued, it led to inaccuracies.

Carroll urged that children should be taken through much preliminary work without the use of notation. He wrote:

"This wonderful power of retention is the glory of the child-mind.

Piano music for children

Memory lies even deeper than habit, and a thing once memorised is worked into the very fabric of the mind." (11)

FOREST FANTASIES (1916)

Two years after the publication of *Sea Idylls*, Carroll issued a set of nine pieces entitled *Forest Fantasies*. Inspired by the poetry of Edmund Spenser, writer of *The Faerie Queene*, and Carroll's memories of a woodland scene in Galloway, these picturesque pieces are similar in their technical and interpretative demands to *Sea Idylls*.

The influence of Grieg is evident as, for example, in these two extracts from "Dwarfs of the Mist":

As in *Sea Idylls*, each piece has a couplet written at the start, suggesting the mood of the music to the young player.

There are many passages of imaginative and colourful harmony, engaging the pupil's attention and imagination, as in number 6, "Garland Dance":

Piano music for children

All of the pieces demand study in clearly-defined legato and staccato playing, and provide a thorough development of varied types of technique, phrasing and pedalling. Opportunities exist for the acquisition of a cantabile tone in the left hand, and the transfer of ideas from one hand to another in number 4, "The Elfin Harp". The following is a facsimile of Carroll's manuscript of the opening bars:

Early work in simple part-playing is incorporated in number 5, "Sprites of the Twilight":

Carroll was particularly fond of this collection of pieces. For the cover and title-page he again utilised the services of Heath Robinson, who produced another superb set of illustrations.

FIRST PIANO LESSONS BOOK 1a: TUNES FROM NATURE (1919)

THIS collection of teaching pieces, published in 1919, contains sixteen short solo pieces and four duets. They approximate, in length

Piano music for children

and style, to the original collection of 1912: *Scenes at a Farm*.

Carroll's original intention was to produce this volume with simplified notation specially for young children, as in the 1912 book. Under pressure from less progressive teachers, he and his publisher withdrew their innovatory ideas and released *Tunes from Nature* with key and time signatures inserted. However, there is a noticeable absence of speed indications.

Verses by H. Lang Jones appear at the start of each piece, as in *Scenes at a Farm*. An introductory poem, "Nature's Music", by the same writer, depicts the beauties of Nature and its musical sounds produced by the sea, the wind, birds and farmyard animals, ending with a prayer:

" The earth is full of music,
  For those with ears to hear.

  And in the world-wide chorus
  I too may bear a part,
  If but the grace be given me
  Of music in my heart."

Much emphasis is placed on the hands playing together, yet independently, with frequent chordal patterns, as in number 1, "Rosy Morning":

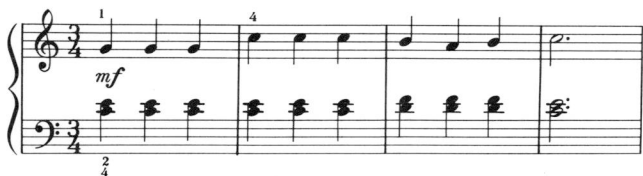

Simple canonic imitation appears in several numbers, including number 14, "Two Green Linnets":

Piano music for children

Expressive markings are somewhat more detailed than in *Scenes at a Farm*. Further, Carroll includes some indications of pedalling. Freer use is made of the chord of the dominant 7th. in this volume, the spread of a 7th. being required in the left hand in six of the pieces. A companion volume to *Scenes at a Farm*, it is slightly more advanced in degree of difficulty, and requires a more mature musical approach.

IN SOUTHERN SEAS (1922)

THIS collection of nine short pieces, subtitled *Nine Miniatures*, appeared in 1922. They were inspired by the life of Robert Louis Stevenson, the Scottish writer who spent the last years of his life on the Pacific island of Samoa.

As in *Sea Idylls* and *Forest Fantasies*, each piece has two lines of poetry to assist the child's imagination and set the scene for the music which follows. Carroll's tempo indications in English reveal a freshness of thought intended to make a direct appeal to children: "Slow, but with airy freshness", "Frisky", "Slowly drifting", and "Feathery". Furthermore, expressive markings during the course of each piece were now frequently in English – an indication of Carroll's concern for his young players.

Each piece is intended to cover one aspect of technique. For example, number 6, "Flakes of Foam", demands accurate, slurred playing of broken chords divided between the hands:

Number 8, "Night's Shining Peace", is a study in sustained legato playing and early training in rubato:

Piano music for children

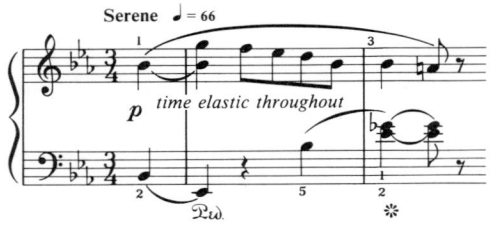

The final – and longest – piece in the collection, "Samoan's Dance", is prefaced by a couplet from Scott:

"His kirtle, made of forest green, reached scantily to his knee;
And, at his belt, of arrows keen a furbished sheaf bore he."

Its principal melody, a study in clear articulation and rhythmic precision, bears traces of folk influence:

The photograph on the front cover of this collection was taken in the Southern Seas, and reproduced in 1922 by permission of the High Commissioner for New Zealand.

MUSICAL EXERCISES (1922)

1922 also saw the publication of *Musical Exercises*, a set of twenty-four short exercises, intended to supplement Carroll's piano pieces in the acquisition of an accomplished and expressive technique. Each exercise deals with a specific technical problem. Carroll claimed that a good exercise has a single object: the task for both teacher and pupil is to discover the objective and to decide how to achieve it.

This set of exercises had appeared, as *First Exercises for Piano*, in the magazine *Music and Youth* throughout 1921. Each exercise is

Piano music for children

accompanied by an informative paragraph giving detailed instructions regarding the object and its attainment. Carroll covers a range of effects, techniques and positions similar to those in *Scenes at a Farm*, though at a more advanced level.

From the first exercise – "Beauty of Tone and Looseness of Arm" – great emphasis is laid on freedom of arm movement, loosely working from the shoulder:

When the looseness of arm has been achieved, the playing of simple chords with a free and comfortable feeling is to be attempted, as in the fifth exercise: "Freedom of Arm in Chord Playing":

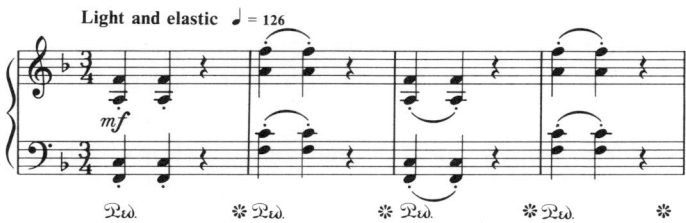

Stress is placed, not only on freedom of arm movement and the production of chords, but also on legato and cantabile playing with an absence of stiffening and the avoidance of uneven playing by careful listening. Exercises in finger-work follow exercises in chord-playing, as in number 7: "Legato for Two Fingers – right hand":

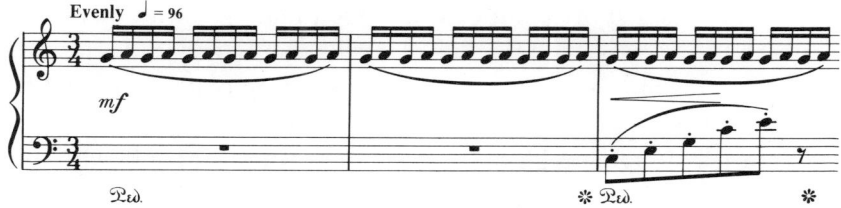

The introduction of chord-playing before finger-work, to avoid stiffness in touch and engage the pupil's interest, evident in these

Piano music for children

Musical Exercises, had been a major point in *Scenes at a Farm*.

Exercises follow to develop ease of movement along the keyboard, wide arched movement in skips with the arm descending from a good height, clean finger-work, freedom from the elbow and thumb joints, and the avoidance of unnecessary movements of finger or hand. Detailed instructions are given on pedalling, and the pupil is exhorted to use the memory as much as possible.

The absence of reliance on purely sequential patterns and the presence of a sharply imaginative musical mind, sympathetic to the needs of teachers and the interests of pupils, bring to these short exercises a variety of textures and expression at once demanding and attractive.

TWELVE STUDIES (1923)

IN his exercises and early pieces, Carroll emphasised the paramount importance of muscular relaxation, freedom and suppleness, in accordance with the ideas of Matthay. All of these compositions reveal his perception of the musical thought of the young child, and display his inventive abilities. The *Twelve Studies*, published in 1923, follow the pattern of those by Bertini, Czerny and Gurlitt, in that they provide pupils with important aspects of piano technique in a reasonably interesting and melodious manner. They had first appeared in *Music and Youth* throughout 1921.

Carroll stated his definition of "Study" in his Preface to *Twelve Studies* as follows:

"A Study is a short composition which makes a kind of bridge between the Exercise and the Piece. It is like an Exercise in one way, because it teaches us to do one particular thing really well, and to know just *how* to do it; and yet a Study can often be played as a piece, because it is long enough and quite interesting to people who are listening."

Carroll did not provide titles for this collection of studies. However, as in the book of *Musical Exercises*, a paragraph of

Piano music for children

commentary, hints and analysis of the problem faced in each piece is presented for the use of teacher and pupil. The set can be described as follows:

1. G major. Loose arm practice utilising the interval of a 6th. to produce a beautiful tone. Moderate speed.

2. C major. A study on quick staccato chords with light touch, in both hands simultaneously. Carroll recommends, at this fast speed, movement from the hand working from the wrist and free arm:

3. C major. Three-note chords, in varied close hand positions, are played alternately between the hands. The left hand crosses over the right hand. Fairly quick.

4. D minor. A flowing study. At the end of each slur, the hands are to be loosely raised:

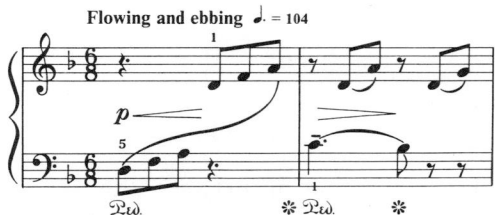

5. E minor. Practice in precise, loose finger-touch. Carroll stresses the aims of neatness and control:

Piano music for children

6. A minor. Another rapid staccato chord study. Carroll recommends that the arms should be neither stiff nor loose, the wrists firm but not stiff, and the hands firm but lively. The fingers, carried by hand and arm along the keys, have little independent action.

7. C major. A study in right-hand leisurely melody with a quiet, rising left-hand accompaniment:

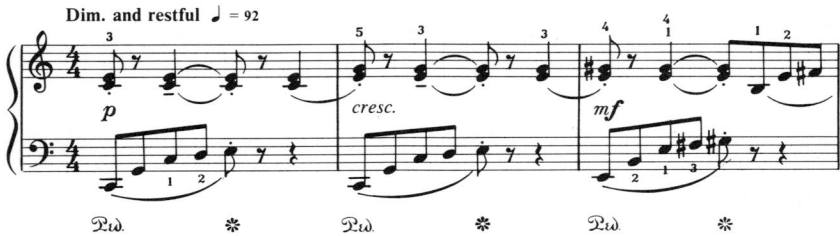

8. D minor. Melody and accompaniment appear in the right hand, over a quaver bass to be played with a free arm movement. The right-hand fingers are to remain close to the keys:

9. G major. A study in chords alternating between the hands, moving up and down the keyboard incorporating many different hand-positions and chromatic notes:

Piano music for children

10. E flat major. A soaring melody in the left hand requiring a full tone, with right-hand accompaniment. Fairly fast.

11. A flat major. A slow study in accurate scale passages divided between the hands.

12. C major. A lively study requiring a free use of the arms in broken chord figurations, divided between the hands:

The *Six Easy Studies in Olden Style*, *Musical Exercises* and *Twelve Studies* compise all of Carroll's published works intended specifically to develop the pupil's technique.

WATER SPRITES (1923)

APPROXIMATING in difficulty to *In Southern Seas*, a collection of twelve descriptive pieces entitled *Water Sprites* was published in 1923. A short verse from poets as diverse as Arnold, Heine and Tennyson appears at the start of each piece, to stimulate the child's imagination.

This collection had been published in the monthly magazine *Music and Youth* throughout 1921.

As in the *Musical Exercises* and *Twelve Studies*, Carroll adds an informative note regarding technique and interpretation of each piece. His opinion regarding the programmatic and imaginative nature of these pieces is stated in the notes to the first piece:

"A piece should always mean *something* to the player, and something to the listener; but the 'something' which it means is never quite the same to different people. This is one way in which music differs from painting. In a real picture certain objects appear and in

Piano music for children

most cases we are sure what they are. Music leaves our thoughts much more free."

Highly finished and effectively written for the instrument, these twelve pieces, each of one page in length, reveal some of Carroll's most imaginative harmonic colouring, requiring accurate note-reading and careful positioning of the hands, as in number 2, "From Sea-Green Caves":

Careful attention to recurring rhythmic figures is required, as in this short extract from number 6, "Mermaid's Lullaby":

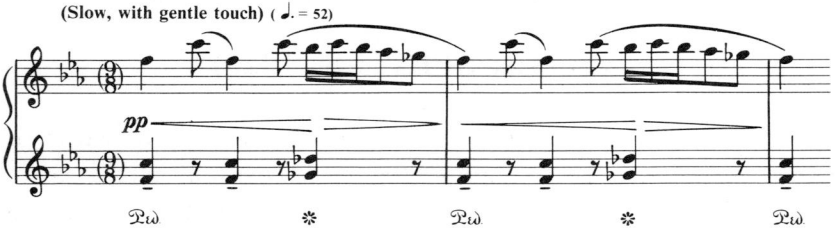

In the same piece, instructions are given to use both pedals:

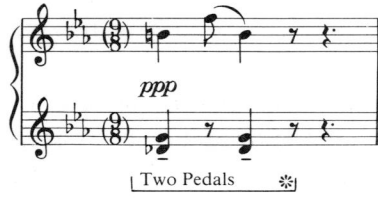

Carroll's notes cover both technical and artistic details, and evoke the spirit or mood of the title in order to engage the pupil's attention. His imaginative tempo indications, as always in English, also serve to encourage and develop the pupil's powers of expression. For example, the opening of number 4, "The Echo Nymph":

Piano music for children

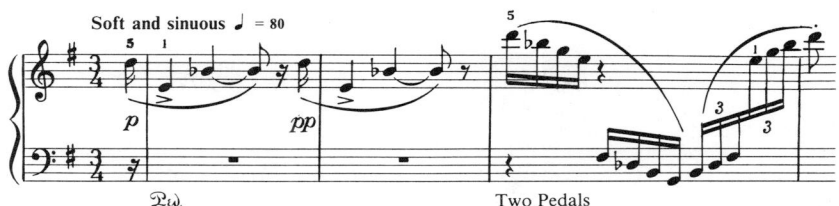

In his pursuit of the co-ordination between music, poetry and drawing, Carroll employed the artist Charles Folkard to design the cover page.

Numbers 4, 6 and 7 from this collection, together with number 8 from *Forest Fantasies* and number 9 from *In Southern Seas*, were orchestrated for flute, oboe, clarinet, bassoon, horn, timpani, triangle and strings by Eric Fogg. Published in 1930 as a *Children's Suite for Small Orchestra*, the orchestral arrangement was entitled *Seascape*.

RIVER AND RAINBOW (1933)

THERE is a gap of ten years, from 1923 to 1933, in Carroll's output of educational compositions. This period covered years when he was fully occupied as Music Adviser to Manchester Education Committee.

In 1933, *River and Rainbow* was published. Clearly, Carroll had retained his unique skills of composing for children. This is a collection of ten short pieces approximating in difficulty to *Forest Fantasies* of 1916. A further similarity is Carroll's adoption of poetic couplets from varied sources at the start of each piece.

An emphasis is placed in this volume on the development of the pupil's powers of tonal expression, ranging from the very subdued opening of number 2, "The Tiger Moth":

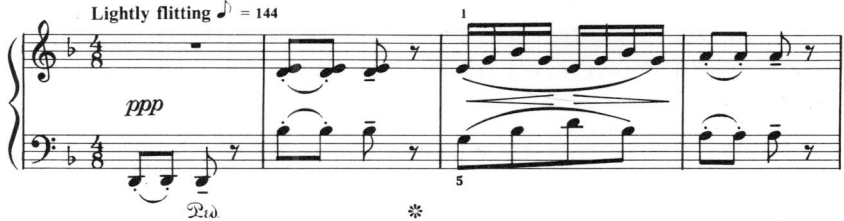

Piano music for children

to the heavy chords at the conclusion of number 7, "Sunrise":

The final piece in the collection, "Ripples", is built on a tiny rippling motif, to be produced by clear finger movement:

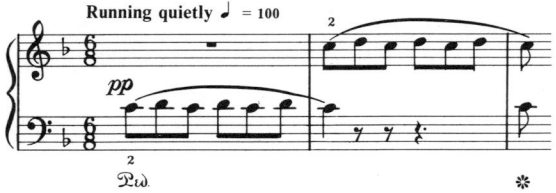

For the cover and title-page Carroll employed the renowned illustrator Arthur Rackham, who shared Carroll's views about the value of imaginative art in the education of young children. This was the only book that Rackham illustrated for Carroll. His detailed "Gothic" style, with its fairies, gnomes and twisted trees, perfectly suited the music. With lovely, delicate colouring, the scene on the cover of the first edition is one of fantasy and enchantment. Rackham wrote to Carroll on 12 June, 1934:

"I am very glad to know you like the result and thank you very sincerely for the appreciation you have expressed. *I* can find fault. But I'd better not."

Carroll and his publishers, Forsyth, had reason to be pleased: these unique Rackham illustrations, and those by Heath Robinson and Folkard, must rank among the finest music covers ever produced.

Piano music for children

FOUR GYPSIES (1937)

THIS suite of four pieces was published by Ricordi of London, three years after Carroll had retired from his post as Manchester's Music Adviser. Although not specifically described as educational pieces for the pianist, these pieces can serve as useful material bridging the gap between *The Countryside* and collections such as *Forest Fantasies* and *Sea Idylls*. Each piece is prefaced by a couplet of poetry, summoning the spirit of the piece and providing an imaginative framework for its technical demands.

For example, the first piece, "Melissa", a simple ternary form structure, demanding a light finger touch, has the following phrase from an old song:

"Nimble her feet as the mountain hind
And darker her hair than the night."

Carroll's aim is to invoke in the player an imaginative response, by technique and sensitivity, to the couplet and the staccato nature of the piece:

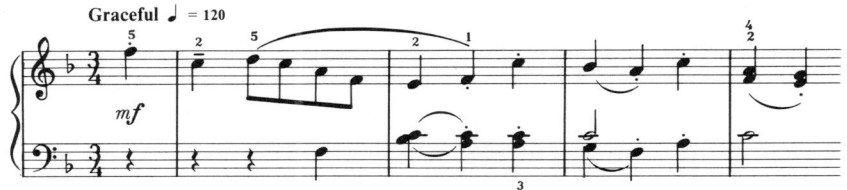

FOUR COUNTRY DANCES (1953)

SIXTEEN years elapsed before the publication of Carroll's next set of piano pieces. This volume, published in 1953 by Forsyth, the publishers of his earliest teaching volumes, appeared forty-one years after *Scenes at a Farm* and forty-five years after *First Lessons in Bach*, Book 1.

1. "Elfinboys." F major. Marked "Merrily", this piece demands a clear distinction between legato and staccato playing, a control of

Piano music for children

tonal variety and dynamics within fairly narrow limits, a delicate balance between a right-hand melody and left-hand accompaniment, and a careful approach to crotchet rests:

2. "The Fairy Ring." C major. Carroll's careful musicianship is evident in this short, playful piece. A melody in the right hand is accompanied by left-hand chords. A short contrasting passage of close, effective imitation in A minor stretches the pupil's co-ordinating powers and develops a feeling for simple counterpoint:

3. "Gnome." E minor. The couplet at the start, by Horne, sets the mood of this short, rapid, staccato piece:

"His limbs are all antics – he skips like a flea;
His body is brown as the bark of a tree."

Right hand and left hand share the main melodic idea, with its emphasis on precise touch, even tone and clear articulation:

Piano music for children

4. "Zephyr." C major. Marked "Buoyant", this final piece contrasts smooth broken-chord figures, using varied hand positions, and short quaver chords. The pupil is required to play flowing arpeggio figures in an unbroken line between the hands but with the occasional crossing of the left hand over the right hand:

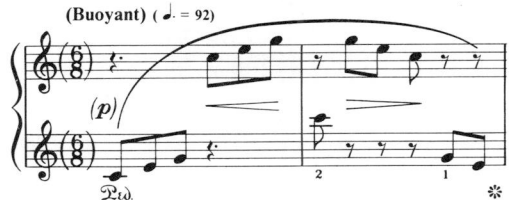

At the conclusion of this volume, Carroll, in an "Afterword", addressed himself, for the final time, to the children who might use his educational volumes of piano music:

"Many years ago the writer decided to make a tour in southern Scotland and so to test the condition of Music in that region which had been the inspiration of so many of his compositions. The result was pleasing and valuable, especially in regard to children and young people, many of them occupants of caravans, and of the dry and accessible cliffs provided by nature.

Music, dancing and poetry were the most perfect features, presented with confidence and by memory. Asked to name poet or composer brought no response. A few bits of paper, hardly readable were offered, but seldom accepted by the visitor, who tried to catch the words as they came. The composer of the music had to make new tunes to fit the poetry and rhythm presented.

Thus ends the little note to the pupil from Walter Carroll."

Carroll's piano-teaching pieces, especially the three books comprising *First Piano Lessons*, were in the forefront of a new age in the education of child pianists. They have affected the outlook and methods of countless teachers and the musical education of several generations of children.

Many other musicians composed pieces specially for child

Piano music for children

beginners in the early years of the twentieth century, adopting principles similar to those of Carroll. As the popularity of piano tutors and methods, utilised so much in the nineteenth century, declined, so the books of descriptive and imaginative pieces rose. A general recognition of the values of close links between life and music, and their application to teaching pieces, stimulating the child's power of self-expression, can be seen in other publications in the first two decades of the century. Carroll's principles of co-ordinating the arts of music, poetry and illustration in the pursuit of suitable teaching material can be discovered in the works of other composers for children.

Among Carroll's contemporaries, Ernest Austin, Thomas Dunhill, Harry Farjeon, Norman O'Neill, Alec Rowley and Felix Swinstead produced pieces for children. In a later generation, Dorothy Bradley, James Ching, Cyril Dalmaine, Leslie Fly, Barbara Kirkby-Mason, Joan Last, John Longmire, Muriel Mungo-Park and Geoffrey Tankard maintained the output of educational piano music, frequently using descriptive titles and stories to excite interest in piano study.

Carroll's piano-teaching pieces, with their clear structure, balance of unity and contrast, variety of key, melodic shapes, harmony and rhythm, together with the undefinable quality of true inspiration, have withstood the erosion of time and fashion. His blending of the arts into a musical world of nature, fantasy and fairy-tale has great meaning for young children learning to play the piano. If survival is a criterion for a piece of music, Carroll's music for children is remarkable. To date over five million copies have been sold throughout the world.

Moving from composing and writing for adults to producing works for children is by no means unique. A parallel can be drawn with the writer Frances Hodgson Burnett, a near-contemporary of his, also born in Manchester. Her early books, for adults, have been totally forgotten, but in a later book, *The Secret Garden*, she produced a children's classic still highly regarded by today's children. Published in 1911, the year before Carroll's *Scenes at a*

Piano music for children

Farm, the illustrations to the first edition were by Charles Robinson, the elder brother of Carroll's famous illustrator.

With deep understanding of the young child's mind, Carroll ranks among the finest twentieth-century composers for children. Not all composers are called on to write lengthy symphonies or dramatic operas. Just as literature has seen the children's fairy tales of Hans Christian Andersen and Oscar Wilde, and the stories of Beatrix Potter, so music has its composers who limit themselves to a smaller field, in which they excel. Such a man was Walter Carroll, the children's composer.

chapter nine

Retirement years

Lectures. *The Enchanted Isle.* Magazine articles. *Music in Life and Education.* Final years.

LECTURES

ON the occasion of his retirement, Carroll is reported to have said: "I mean to work harder than ever – lecturing, composing, writing and *living!*" (1) During these later years, he took a fine studio at 9 Albert Square, Manchester, but found it very lonely compared with the Education Offices in Deansgate.

From 1920, the year of his full-time appointment as Manchester's Music Adviser, to 1944, when he was aged 75, he gave at least 443 lectures, generally in the evenings or on Saturday afternoons, to education and music associations, education authorities and holiday courses. Travelling entirely by public transport, as he never owned a car, he visited the surrounding districts of Manchester, and towns throughout England, Scotland and Wales.

In 1935, the year after his retirement, he gave no fewer than forty-six lectures, including towns as diverse as Bexhill, Birmingham, Chester-le-Street, Durham, Exeter, Glasgow, Middlesbrough and Nuneaton. He lectured frequently in Wales from 1936, including courses for the University of Wales Council of Music. Other towns in which he lectured during his retirement were Edinburgh and

Retirement years

Plymouth in 1936, Blackburn and Rochdale in 1937, and Nottingham, Oldham, Southport and Stretford during the years 1938 to 1944. These lectures, like his earlier ones, were always well attended. His thoughtful personality, high level of communication skills and enthusiasm, together with snatches of humour, caught the attention and have lived in the memories of his audiences.

In his lecture, *The Organisation of Music in a School*, given several times in 1935, Carroll drew on his vast experience in education. He aimed to help and encourage, to widen the personal outlook, to improve former teaching methods and to discuss new methods. He saw music as a force in the training of character: therefore, the aims should be educative not competitive, in order to establish permanent standards not subject to fashion.

The essential subject in the music curriculum, because of its ability to develop children from within, was singing, with its three components of voice-training, aural work and sight-reading. Optional subjects were musical appreciation, with its cultural value, music-making, with its inventive value, and choral and orchestral work, with their emphasis on co-operation.

His *Handbook of Music* and *The Training of Children's Voices* were used in this, and other lectures, as a basis for explanation and discussion. Members present at his lectures were referred to his published lists of recommended songs as suitable material.

Constant references in his lectures to the natural musical possessions of children and the need to cultivate them early in the child's life, in a systematic manner, incorporating action songs, singing games, nursery tunes and folk-material, invite comparison with the work of three later foreign music educators, Zoltán Kodály of Hungary, Carl Orff of Germany and Shinichi Suzuki of Japan.

Carroll's record of his lectures ceases with a lecture, *Voice in Speech and Song*, given to the Organists' Association at Oldham on 12 February, 1944. During the war years, 1939–1945, he taught at Holy Innocents School, Fallowfield, Manchester, as an emergency supply teacher on a voluntary basis.

Retirement years

VIOLIN TEACHING ALBUM, THE ENCHANTED ISLE (1946)

AT the age of 71, six years after he had retired, Carroll moved into a new educational field and wrote a set of pieces, entitled *The Enchanted Isle*, for children learning to play the violin. In order to accomplish this successfully, he taught himself the preliminary stages of playing the instrument.

There are ten short pieces, with piano accompaniment, in *The Enchanted Isle*. As well as descriptive titles, all the pieces have a couplet of poetry at the start to stimulate the pupil's imagination. The pieces are as carefully contrasted in mood and expression and as meticulously constructed as the piano-teaching pieces. Detailed bowing, dynamic and expressive markings, together with varied and closely integrated accompaniments, are intended to develop the powers of expression and interpretation.

    1. "Dawn at Sea." A major. Separate bows; the note-values are crotchets and minims:

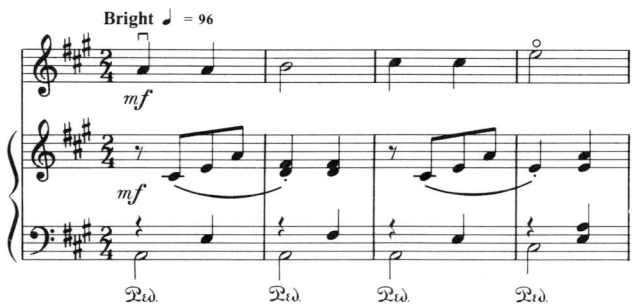

    2. "Smooth Waters." A major. An expressive, calm piece demanding careful control of bowing and intonation. Similar in range to "Dawn at Sea".

    3. "There Lies the Land." D major. An energetic piece, mainly in crotchet movement, with detailed dynamic shadings. The opening melody:

Retirement years

is repeated in the sixth bar, a 5th. higher, developing the child's aural skills, intonation and appreciation of formal structure:

4. "Island Legend." A minor. A sad piece, similar in range, style and technical demands to "Smooth Waters".

5. "The Silver Stream." E major. Emphasis is on the four fingers on the E string. A flowing piano accompaniment supports a melody demanding careful listening and accurate positioning on the fingerboard.

6. "At Sunset." G major. The G string is incorporated for the first time in the collection. Slurred quavers appear as a unifying idea, requiring careful bowing and accurate rhythm:

7. "Moon Sprites." A minor. A delicate waltz, requiring careful distinction between F and F sharp, C and C sharp. The last four bars incorporate pizzicato playing, at the discretion of the teacher.

8. "Siesta." F major. Compound triple time. The rhythm of the opening figure appears throughout the piece, the three quavers always being placed on the third beat:

117

Retirement years

9. "The Rock Temple." D major. Much use is made of the figure ♩. ♫ ♩. To assist the young violinist in the performance of this figure, it appears also in the piano accompaniment – at first with the violinist, then in simple dialogue:

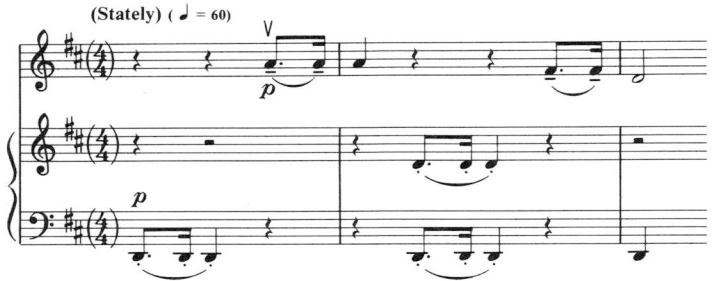

10. "Singhalese Dancer." The final piece is in E minor, simple compound time. Carroll uses the same motifs at different levels of pitch to develop the child's intonation and technique. The opening figure:

appears later as:

When the pieces were completed, Carroll contacted Heath Robinson again for a cover design and title-page. Heath Robinson was keen to do exactly what Carroll required in the details, down to the ages of the children in the sketches and the manner of holding the musical instruments. The result was a dreamlike and beautiful portrayal of children and nature.

They decided to wait until after the War had ended before going into publication: the collection appeared in 1946. Unfortunately, Heath Robinson died two years before then. In a letter to Carroll dated 27 September, 1944, Heath Robinson's widow wrote to say

Retirement years

how much her husband had enjoyed working with Carroll, and expressed the wish that people would know more of her husband's serious art as well as his "Heath Robinson contraptions" of strange, ingenious machinery. This collaboration between musician and artist had spanned thirty years. They had a great regard for each other's creations and similar views concerning the power of the child's imagination. From a business relationship there developed a strong friendship.

The principles and methods, involving an integrated approach to learning a musical instrument, a direct appeal to the imagination of the child, an emphasis on the latent powers of expression, the development of technical proficiency by pieces rather than repetitive exercises, and an overriding regard for musicianship and aural perception, which had formed the basis of Carroll's piano-teaching pieces, were now transformed to violin teaching.

MAGAZINE ARTICLES

In the 1920s, Carroll was a member of the Editorial Board of the magazine, *Music and Youth*. In 1922, he contributed four short articles to the magazine – "Thoroughness", "Memory", "Imagination" and "Expression".

From September 1939 to October 1940, the other major British magazine for music teachers, *Music in Schools*, published seven articles on music education by Carroll:

1. Seven Lamps of a Child's Mind.
2. Music and the Young Child.
3. Voice in Speech and Song (from 3 to 7 years).
4. Voice in Speech and Song (from 8 years onward).
5. Sounds and Symbols.
6. Songs of Youth.
7. The Building of a Choir.

Retirement years

MUSIC IN LIFE AND EDUCATION (1948)

CARROLL'S articles from *Music in Schools*, and other writings, were gathered together in a volume, *Music in Life and Education*, published in 1948.

The first part of this short book concludes with an essay, "Music in Education", in which Carroll summarises his beliefs in the field of music education of young children. He is quite definite in the value he placed on the earliest years: "In the whole range of training there is no phase quite so fruitful in results as the time spent in the Infants' School." (2) He stresses again that both tonic sol-fa and staff notation should be taught from the earliest stages together, and that at every stage sounds should precede signs.

The basic aim of music education should be the unfolding of a sense of beauty already present in the child; the interest and enjoyment thus built up is a valuable lifelong possession. In order to achieve this absorption and enjoyment of music, he suggests that by the upper classes of the junior school, one third of the music curriculum should consist of music appreciation lessons.

Part two of this volume, entitled "The Story of Music", outlines ten early lessons in musical appreciation. The Postscript is among Carroll's final published writings. It concludes:

"Music in Education still needs great leaders, gifted organizers and inspiring teachers. In the future it has to play a vital part as a link between peoples and nations. It needs neither politics nor propaganda, for its service is that of spreading a spirit of union and goodwill – surely a mission deserving of priority among the world problems of today."

FINAL YEARS

AT the end of the Second World War, Carroll's health went into a rapid and sudden decline, not, ironically, owing to his old heart ailment, but to a muscular disease resulting in the loss of movement and strength in his legs. Quickly losing confidence, he gave up going

Retirement years

out of the home, and within a short time became bedfast. He remained so for the last ten years of his life, cared for by his devoted wife and daughters.

During these years he had a continual stream of visitors, often in a rota drawn up by Ida. Among his closest friends in these final years were the Methodist, Robert Lee, and his two former colleagues, Gertrude Riall and Dennis Chapman. His faithful secretary, Wilhemina Davies, arrived two or three times a week to deal with his correspondence; she died on the day following Carroll's death.

Visitors were greeted with joy, and often left with a small gift – a book, a poem or a translation of a German song. He rarely talked about his illness, but remained interested in other people, their careers and aspirations, and kept in contact with day-to-day events outside his home. He was a careful listener, possessing a tolerance so strong that nothing would shock him, and revealed an ability to get to the heart of matters. Very frail, thin and pale, he showed a fighting spirit during this long illness; years of single-minded campaigning and tireless dedication had prepared him well. He remained mentally active throughout, reading a great deal, playing chess and retaining his quiet, natural humour.

Younger visitors were received with particular pleasure. Dorothy Pilling remarked that "he knew the basic things of personality; he didn't get sidetracked by irrelevancies. He was very sympathetic and understanding." Irene Wilde remembers him "with affection and gratitude for his help and good advice on many occasions . . . his genuine love for young people and his sensitivity to their hopes and ideas . . . to those people who were fortunate to know him personally he must always remain a living memory of a great friend and a devoted musician."

In 1951, when he was aged 82, Carroll published a short booklet, *The True Story of Scenes at a Farm and other Music of Nature composed by Walter Carroll*. It describes how he wrote the teaching pieces almost forty years earlier.

Among the many letters of appreciation and goodwill which he received in his final years, the following extract from a letter from

Retirement years

the Lord Mayor of Manchester, dated 25 June, 1948, expressed the feelings of many of his fellow citizens:

". . . I may say how splendidly and usefully you have shaped your life and what a help you must have been to many young teachers. How right you are about having to 'go up' rather than 'come down' to children."

The Bishop of Hereford, Richard Godfrey Parsons, who had been Rector of St. James's Church, Birch, during Carroll's years as Choirmaster there, wrote to him on 21 October, 1948. He referred to Carroll's new book, *Music in Life and Education*, saying:

"the earliest essays I have read with an inner sympathy for your valiant defence of the supremacy of the spiritual, and your insistence on the unity – but not uniformity – of its essential elements . . . I look back on our years together at Birch with much gratitude for all you did for the Church and for myself."

In a communication of November 1953, Percy A. Scholes, fellow pioneer in the field of teaching music appreciation to children, wrote "To my valued old friend Dr. Walter Carroll whose great work for Musical Education I much admire."

On the occasion of his 85th birthday – 4 July, 1954 – Carroll received a short letter from Gertrude Riall, which must have brought him particular pleasure:

"My Dear Friend,

Today you have completed 85 years – and begin another span tomorrow – just twenty years since you left the office in Deansgate – it doesn't seem so long – I remember so clearly the events of your period of office, and the stamp of Walter Carroll is still in the schools . . .

With love from your old assistant,
Gertrude R."

These four letters – from the chief citizen of Manchester, an Anglican bishop, a fellow progressive in music education, and a

Retirement years

former colleague – testify to the valued friendship of Carroll, to the respect in which he was held and to the breadth of his influence.

Walter Carroll died, at the age of 86, on 9 October, 1955, at his home in Lapwing Lane. The Vice-Chancellor of Manchester University, J. S. B. Stopford, wrote to Gertrude Carroll: "Manchester is heavily in his debt and will ever be proud of what he was able to achieve."

In 1956, an anonymous donor presented the Northern School of Music with £2,000, to establish a scholarship in Carroll's memory. Gertrude Carroll outlived her husband by just three years, dying on 16 November, 1958, at the age of 90.

On 23 May, 1959, a Service of Dedication of a Walter Carroll Memorial Window took place in the Musicians' Memorial Chapel of the Church of St. Sepulchre, Holborn, London. The service was conducted by the Dean of St. Paul's Cathedral. Carroll's own anthem, *Sleep thy Last Sleep*, was sung by the Choir of the Stationers' Company's School.

A Service of Commemoration of the centenary of Carroll's birth was held in the same chapel on 6 July, 1969. The Choir, from the Northern School of Music, sang music by Mozart, Schubert, Howells and Balfour Gardiner. Fittingly, prayers were offered for world peace, a cause to which Carroll had been devoted. In his address Dr. Charles Thornton Lofthouse, a former pupil of Carroll's, spoke of him as:

"a man of great humility . . . He treated his students and those with whom he came in contact with dignity and respect. By doing so, he drew out from those of us who were under him more than we thought it possible to attain . . . His great points were the proper musical education of the young, and an intelligent standard of teaching in the schools."

chapter ten

Summing up

BRITISH music educators during the final decades of the nineteenth century and the first half of the twentieth century were frequently associated with a specialist branch of the subject. Macpherson and Scholes are identified with the musical appreciation movement, Annie Curwen and Matthay with teaching the piano, Parry and Stanford with university teaching, and Walford Davies with wireless broadcasts on music specially for adults.

Walter Carroll's work was memorable and unusual in its range, quality and influence, embracing many aspects of music education. To his pioneer work in the training of music teachers at the Manchester Day Training College and the Royal Manchester College of Music, and as the country's first full-time Music Adviser, must be added his lectureships in harmony and musical composition at the Victoria University of Manchester and the Royal Manchester College of Music. His active membership of public associations in the forefront of the collective expression of the music profession, such as the Incorporated Society of Musicians, contrasts with his own unique private venture, his Training Class for Music Teachers. His generous support, during his retirement years, for the developing Matthay School, with its emphasis on the training of teachers, is set alongside his years as Director of Music at St. James's Church, Birch, his published works on the training of children's voices, notes and booklets for advanced music students, his essays

Summing up

on music education and his lectures throughout England, Scotland and Wales.

His work from 1918 with the Manchester Elementary Schools' Choir, Schoolchildren's Orchestra, and series of concerts designed for children, found its parallel in similar ventures in other parts of the country, including Bristol, Liverpool and London. However, none appears to have been attempted on such a scale, and with such thoroughness, as Carroll's. The joint performances of the Elementary Schools' Choir and the Hallé Orchestra, an international orchestra under the celebrated composer and conductor Hamilton Harty, were singular events in the lives of Manchester schoolchildren, and have few parallels in the field of music education. The production of their gramophone recording of 1929, a unique event in the history of recording, has no parallel, and remains a permanent legacy.

Many education authorities and advisory staff, at home and abroad, thousands of teachers and several generations of schoolchildren came under Carroll's direct influence through his courses, writings, music and lectures.

Carroll's first post was a teaching post, at the Manchester Day Training College from 1892. Throughout the rest of his long and active life he continued to follow the progress of music courses at training colleges, particularly as they affected the supply and quality of teachers of young children. His views remained consistent, strongly held and, when necessary, forcibly expressed.

Carroll's concern for the training of music teachers and the teaching of music in infant and primary schools was based largely on his own study of children. He also studied and wrote about the philosophy and methods of other teachers – Froebel, Pestalozzi, John Curwen, Annie Curwen and Matthay. When he entered the field of education in 1892, the concept of education was limited, allotting little time to the teaching of music or the training of music teachers. Forty years later, outstanding developments had taken place, with Carroll in the forefront. Many local education authorities, including Manchester, London, Cardiff and Sheffield,

Summing up

were supporting broader schemes of music education with enthusiasm and financial help.

The changes in emphasis in school music teaching did not come about by chance, but owing to the work of pioneers such as Walter Carroll. Such detailed schemes as he produced for the schools of Manchester, with special emphasis on the primary sector, are rare in British music education even today.

Carroll's career had followed a remarkable course. From an unprivileged background, lacking strong musical traditions, he was among the first to be awarded the degree of Mus.B. at Durham University, the first Mus.D. by examination at Manchester University, the first lecturer in music at the Manchester Day Training College and the first Professor of the Art of Teaching at the Royal Manchester College of Music. At the height of his academic success he devoted himself to the musical needs of the poor, underprivileged children of Manchester as their first Music Adviser. He joined the struggle for educational advance, for the cultural sensibilities of countless Manchester schoolchildren, to whom he gave skills and confidence, a belief in hard work, co-operation and self-reliance. A fine, clear-sighted administrator, he gathered around him in his years as Music Adviser a group of gifted staff who applied their own skills and energies to his progressive music schemes.

Carroll did not shrink from making a stand on matters of principle – for example, his resignation from the Incorporated Society of Musicians. He challenged orthodox thinking in music education of his day. During his years at St. James's Church, Birch, he supported the right of women choir members to wear surplices. In 1935, he attacked the Hallé Orchestra's policy of discrimination in its exclusion of women players. (1)

Carroll's views on the value of music in education can best be summarised in a passage from a lecture he delivered in 1910:

"Music should not be regarded as an embodiment of physical effort. It should be taught, and practised, for its refining and ennobling power – a product of Mind and Heart – a lever which

Summing up

helps to bring the human into closer touch with the Divine." (2)

Insistent on high standards, meticulous in preparation and presentation, Carroll was a commanding figure in music education. A man of faith and vision, with a deep love and understanding of children, he stressed the importance of family life, the better side of man's nature, a concern for world affairs, frequently turning to the scriptures for guidance.

The aspect of Walter Carroll's work which sets him apart from his contemporaries was his achievement as a truly creative educationist, revealed above all in his series of original piano-teaching albums with their child-centred approach. The significance of Walter Carroll for today lies in his expression of a belief in the value of music education for all children, the cultivation of musical skills and appreciation, and the unremitting pursuit of high ideals.

Glenluce has remained the family home for Carroll's daughters. Following their father's example of concern, hospitality and service, they give their lives to a busy routine of educational and musical schemes, and charitable work, playing a major part in the Abbeyfield Society, the national charity supporting homes for the elderly. In 1963, they donated the adjoining house to *Glenluce* to be an Abbeyfield Home. A blue plaque is affixed to the front of their home. It reads: "Walter Carroll – 1869–1955 – Musician and Composer – Lived Here." His lasting monument lies in his music for children.

Notes

Chapter One
1. *The School Music Review*, 1 June, 1899, p.17. Stainer's complete report was reprinted in this periodical in May and June 1899.
2. Letter from Brodsky to Elgar dated 5 April, 1904, quoted in Michael Kennedy, *The History of the Royal Manchester College of Music*, (Manchester: University Press, 1971), p.30.
3. *The Department of Education in the University of Manchester 1890-1911*, (Manchester: University Press, 1911), p.59.

Chapter Two
1. Carroll, *The Training of Music Teachers*, (No publisher given, 1907), p.9.
2. ibid., p.16.
3. I.S.M., *Monthly Report*, July 1910, p.394.

Chapter Three
1. Carroll's opening announcement for the session 1908-1909.
2. *Manchester City News*, 26 March, 1910, p.3.
3. Carroll: General letter to Editor of Music Journals, n.d.
4. Carroll, *The Unfolding of Personality*, (Manchester: Sherratt and Hughes, 1914), p.4.
5. ibid., pp.6-7.

Chapter Four
1. *The Manchester City News*, 2 April, 1910, p.8.
2. Carroll, *Outlines of Art of Teaching Lectures at the Royal Manchester College of Music*, (Typewritten by J. S. Halliwell, 1920), p.21.
3. Royal Manchester College of Music, *17th Annual Report of Council, 1910*, p.13.
4. Royal Manchester College of Music, *20th Annual Report of Council, 1913*, p.10.
5. *The Manchester Guardian*, 1 December, 1917, p.8.
6. ibid., p.8.
7. ibid., p.8.

Notes

Chapter Five
1. Carroll, *Report to Manchester Education Committee*, September 1918, p.10.
2. Manchester Education Committee, *General Survey 1914-1924*, (Manchester: Education Committee, 1926), p.80.
3. ibid., pp.80-81.
4. Carroll, *Music in Manchester Schools: 1918-1930*, (Manchester: Education Committee, 1930), p.6.
5. ibid., p.39.
6. ibid., p.39.
7. Carroll, *The Training of Children's Voices*, (Manchester: Forsyth, 1922), p.18.
8. Carroll, *A Great Adventure*, unpublished essay, n.d., p.4.
9. Carroll, *Scheme for the Development of Music in Manchester Schools*, December 1920, p.5.
10. Carroll, *Report to Manchester Education Committee*, 1924, p.3.
11. Carroll, *Report to Manchester Education Committee*, September 1931, p.4.
12. Carroll, *The Place of Music in Education*, (Typewritten address, 4 January, 1924), p.1.
13. "The Musician's Bookshelf" in *The School Music Review*, 15 June, 1925, p.13.
14. Mrs. E. Hall (née Edna Jamieson) interviewed by the present writer, 9 June, 1981.
15. Carroll, *Report to Manchester Education Committee*, December 1928, p.2.
16. Carroll, *Music in Manchester Schools: 1918-1930*, p.35.
17. Alan Hulme in *Manchester Evening News*, 19 June, 1975, p.11.
18. *The Music Teacher*, March 1930, p.146.
19. British Broadcasting Corporation radio programme on the occasion of the Fiftieth Reunion of the Manchester Elementary Schoolchildren's Choir, 1975.
20. *The Guardian*, 18 June, 1975, p.24.
21. *The Daily Telegraph*, 19 June, 1975, p.17.
22. Carroll, *Music in Manchester Schools: 1918-1930*, p.40.
23. ibid., p.12.
24. Carroll, *Report to Manchester Education Committee*, September 1931, p.1.
25. *Times Educational Supplement*, 23 August, 1930, p.366.
26. *The Manchester City News*, 8 December, 1928, p.6.

Chapter Six
1. *Magazine of the Matthay School, Manchester*, 1939, p.6.
2. *Magazine of the Matthay School, Manchester*, 1940, p.5.
3. *Magazine of the Matthay School, Manchester*, 1942, p.6.
4. *Magazine of the Northern School of Music*, 1950, p.3.
5. ibid., p.4.

Chapter Seven
1. *Quarterly Record of the National Union of Organists*, January 1923, p.37.
2. Carroll, *The Training of a Voluntary Choir*, typewritten lecture, 1926, p.2.
3. ibid., p.7.

Chapter Eight
1. Robert Roberts, *The Classic Slum*, (Harmondsworth: Penguin Books, 1973), p.32.

Notes

2. Carroll, Preface to *First Lessons in Bach*, Book 1, (Manchester: Forsyth, 1908).
3. Carroll, *The Musical Education of Ida G. Carroll*, handwritten booklet, n.d.
4. Carroll, *The True Story of 'Scenes at a Farm' and other music of nature composed by Walter Carroll*, (Manchester: Forsyth, 1951), p.9.
5. Carroll, Preface to *Scenes at a Farm*, (Manchester: Forsyth, 1912).
6. Carroll, *Notes on the Teaching of First Piano Lessons*, (Manchester: Forsyth, 1912), p.12.
7. ibid., p.13.
8. Carroll, *The True Story of 'Scenes at a Farm'*, p.17.
9. Carroll, Preface to *Sea Idylls*, (Manchester: Forsyth, 1914).
10. Carroll, *First Lessons to the Young*, handwritten booklet, n.d., pp.21-22.
11. ibid.

Chapter Nine
1. *The Music Teacher*, January 1934, p.313.
2. Carroll, *Music in Life and Education*, (London: Joseph Williams, 1948), p.45.

Chapter Ten
1. *Musical Opinion and Music Trades Review*, February 1935, p.422.
2. Carroll, *The Training of the Imagination*, handwritten lecture, 1910, p.28.

The published works of Walter Carroll

Title	Date	Publisher
Two Sonatinas. (1)	1892	Forsyth
When Jesus Christ Our Lord was Born.	1893	Curwen
Advice to Students Preparing for Examination in the Theory of Music.	1894	Heywood
Single Chant in C.	1899	Bristol tune-book
Manchester Time and Tune: Exercises for the Use of Singing and Harmony Classes.	1900	Curwen
Fallowfield.	1901	Sheffield Sunday School Union
Two Hymn Tunes.	1901	Broadbent
ed. Gordon Saunders, Examples in Strict Counterpoint (Old and New), Primer number 41A.	1901	Novello
Magnificat and Nunc Dimittis in F.	1902	Weekes
Benedicite, Omnia Opera, or The Song of the Three Holy Children.	1902	Weekes
Floreat Ellerslie.	1902	Weekes
Hail, Bounteous May.	1902	Bayley and Ferguson
Chorale, Sleep Thy Last Sleep.	1903?	Weekes
Jubilate Deo in F.	1903	Weekes
Te Deum Laudamus in F.	1903	Weekes
Au Bord de la Mer. (2)	1903?	Donajowski
The Study of Music.	1904	Sherratt and Hughes
As Falls the Silent Dew.	1904?	Weekes
Notes on Musical Form. (3)	1906	Sherratt and Hughes
The Teaching of Music.	1906	Sherratt and Hughes
The Training of Music Teachers.	1907	No publisher given
First Lessons in Bach, Book 1.	1908	Forsyth
First Lessons in Bach, Book 2.	1909	Forsyth

The published works of Walter Carroll

Arrangement of the Gigue from Corelli's Sonata in A minor for violin and continuo.	1910	Forsyth
Arrangement of the Allegro from Handel's Harpsichord Suite number 7 in G minor.	1911	Forsyth
Arrangement of Kirnberger's Two-part Fugue in D.	1912	Forsyth
First Piano Lessons, Book 1: Scenes at a Farm.	1912	Forsyth
Notes on First Piano Lessons.	1912	Forsyth
First Piano Lessons, Book 2: The Countryside.	1913	Forsyth
The Unfolding of Personality.	1914	Sherratt and Hughes
Sea Idylls.	1914	Forsyth
Six Easy Studies in Olden Style.	1914	Forsyth
Slumber Song.	1915	Forsyth
Forest Fantasies.	1916	Forsyth
First Piano Lessons, Book 1a: Tunes from Nature.	1919	Forsyth
One Hundred and Fifty Melodies for the Use of Elementary Harmony and Singing Students.	1919	Forsyth
In Southern Seas.	1922	Forsyth
The Training of Children's Voices.	1922	Forsyth
Musical Exercises.	1922	Forsyth
Twelve Studies.	1923	Forsyth
Anthem, Sleep Thy Last Sleep.	1923	Novello
Water Sprites.	1923	Forsyth
Handbook of Music. (4)	1925	Education Committee, Manchester
Music in Manchester Schools.	1930	Education Committee, Manchester
Seascape, arrangements for orchestra by Eric Fogg.	1930	Forsyth
River and Rainbow.	1933	Forsyth
Lord of Our Being. An arrangement of "Sorge nel petto" from Handel's opera Rinaldo, for two-part voices.	1933	Novello
Four Gypsies.	1937	Ricordi
The Unfolding of Personality.	1942	No publisher given. Printed by A. Grayson of Manchester
The Enchanted Isle.	1946	Forsyth
Music in Life and Education.	1948	Williams
The True Story of "Scenes at a Farm".	1951	Forsyth
Four Country Dances.	1953	Forsyth
The Lonely Shepherd, a posthumous publication of piano duets from the earlier volumes of piano-teaching pieces.	1973	Forsyth

The published works of Walter Carroll

Children's Voices: The Fourteen Points of Voice Training.   n.d.   Forsyth

The present writer has been unable to trace the following items from the above list, although they appear in Carroll's own list of works:
When Jesus Christ Our Lord Was Born.
Fallowfield.
Two Hymn Tunes.
Hail, Bounteous May.
Handbook of Music. 1927 edition.

(1) Published in 1914 as *Six Easy Studies in Olden Style.*
(2) Published in 1917 by Forsyth.
(3) Published in 1926 by Forsyth.
(4) Reprinted in 1927 and 1934.

3. PERIODICALS AND NEWSPAPERS
Reference has been made to one or more editions of the following journals:
British Music Society Bulletin.
The Chesterian.
The Choir.
The Daily Telegraph.
The Dominant.
The Guardian.
The Journal of Education.
Manchester and Salford Woman Citizen.
The Manchester City News.
The Manchester Courier and Lancashire General Advertiser.
The Manchester Evening News.
The Minim.
The Monthly Musical Record.
Music and Letters.
Music and Youth.
Music in Education.
Music in Schools.
The Music Student.
The Music Teacher.
The Musical Herald.
The Musical Mirror.
The Musical News.
Musical News and Herald.
Musical Opinion and Music Trades Review.
The Musical Standard.
The Musical Times.
The Musical World.
The Musician.
The Organist and Choirmaster.
The Piano Student.
Pitman's Musical Monthly.

The published works of Walter Carroll

The Quarterly Musical Review.
The Sackbut.
The School Music Review.
Song and Speech.
The Strand Musical Magazine.
The Times.
The Times Educational Supplement.
The Tonic Sol-fa Reporter.
Youth and Music.

A short collection of newspaper cuttings can be found in the Local History Library, Manchester: f 942. 73389 Sc 1.

Bibliography

1. ORIGINAL RECORD SOURCES, OFFICIAL PUBLICATIONS AND REPORTS

Amalgamated Musician's Union: *Musician's Report and Journal.*
Board of Education: *Educational Pamphlets, No.55, Report on Music, Arts and Crafts and Drama in Training Colleges.* 1928.
Board of Education: *Pamphlet 95, Recent Developments in School Music.* 1933.
Board of Education: *Report of the Consultative Committee on the Education of the Adolescent.* 1926.
Board of Education: *Report of the Consultative Committee on the Primary School.* 1931.
Board of Education: *Report of the Departmental Committee on the Training of Teachers for Public Elementary Schools.* 1925.
Board of Education: *Suggestions for the Consideration of Teachers and Others Concerned in the Work of Public Elementary Schools.* 1905; 1927; 1937.
Board of Education: *Suggestions for the Teaching of Singing.* 1914.
British Music: *A Report by the Adult Education Committee on the Development of Adult Education through Music, being Paper No.5 of the Committee.* London: H.M.S.O. 1924.
The Cambridgeshire Report on the Teaching of Music: *Music and the Community.* Cambridge: University Press. 1933.
City of Manchester Charter Centenary Celebrations 1938: *The Work of the Education Committee.* Manchester: Education Committee. 1938.
City of Manchester: *School Board Reports.*
The College of Organists, later the Royal College of Organists: *Prospectuses; Annual Reports.*
Incorporated Society of Musicians: *Bye Laws and Registers of Members; Handbooks; Monthly Reports; Periodical Reports.*
Manchester Education Committee: *Annual Reports; Official Manuals.*
Manchester Education Committee: *Curricula for Public Elementary Schools.* 1906.
Manchester Education Committee: *Education in Manchester; A Survey of Progress 1924–1934.* 1935.

Bibliography

Manchester Education Committee: *Education Week Handbook.* 1924.
Manchester Education Committee: *General Survey 1914–1924.* 1926.
Manchester Education Committee: *Report on the Use in Manchester Schools of (a) Wireless (b) Films.* 1935. (A typewritten pamphlet).
Manchester Education Committee: *Supply and Preliminary Education of Intending Teachers in Manchester.* 1922.
Matthay School of Music, later the Northern School of Music, Manchester: *Magazines.*
Music: a Report on Musical Life in England. London: The Arts Enquiry, P.E.P. 1949.
National Union of Organists: *Quarterly Records.*
Owens College, Manchester: *Calendars.*
Owens College, Manchester: *Magazines.*
Reports of the Committee of Council on Education 1872–1873.
Reports on the Examination in Music of the Students of Training Colleges in England and Wales, from 1892.
Royal Manchester College of Music: *Annual Reports of Council; Calendars; Prospectuses.*
Royal Musical Association Papers 1874–1944.
Victoria University of Manchester: *Calendars.*
Victoria University of Manchester: *The Department of Education in the University of Manchester 1890–1911.*
Victoria University of Manchester: *Minute Book of Proceedings of the Board of the Faculty of Music.*
Victoria University of Manchester: *Outlines of Education Courses at Manchester University.* 1911.
Victoria University of Manchester: *Register of Graduates up to 1 July, 1908.* Manchester: University Press. 1908.

2. BOOKS

Adams, John, editor. *The New Teaching.* London: Hodder and Stoughton. 1919.
Ahrens, Cora B. and G. D. Atkinson. *For All Piano Teachers.* Ontario: The Frederick Harris Music Company. 1955.
Beringer, Oscar. *Fifty Years' Experience of Piano Teaching and Playing.* London: Bosworth. 1908.
Borland, John E. *Musical Foundations: a Record of Musical Work in Schools and Training Colleges, and a Comprehensive Guide for Teachers of School Music.* London: Oxford University Press. 1927.
British Association for the Advancement of Science. *Manchester and its Region.* Manchester: University Press. 1962.
Brocklehurst, B. J. *Music in Schools.* London: Routledge and Kegan Paul. 1962.
Brown, James D. and Stephen S. Stratton. *British Musical Biography.* New York: Da Capo Press. 1971.
Buck, Percy C. *Psychology for Musicians.* London: Oxford University Press. 1944.
Cardus, Neville. *Second Innings.* London: Collins. 1950.
Charlton, H. B. *Portrait of a University 1851–1951.* Manchester: University Press. 1951.
Charlton, Peter. *The Development of Musical Appreciation in Secondary Schools in England, 1900–1950.* Unpublished M.Ed. thesis. University of Leicester. 1971.

Bibliography

Colles, H. C. *The Royal College of Music 1883–1933.* London: Macmillan. 1933.
Corder, Frederick. *A History of the Royal Academy of Music from 1822 to 1922.* London: Anglo-French. 1922.
Curtis, S. J. *History of Education in Great Britain.* London: University Tutorial Press. 1968.
Curwen, Mrs. J. Spencer. *Psychology Applied to Music Teaching.* London: Curwen. 1920.
Dent, H. C. *1870–1970 Century of Growth in English Education.* London: Longmans. 1970.
The Department of Education in the University of Manchester 1890–1911. Manchester: University Press. 1911.
Ehrlich, C. *The Piano: a History.* London: Dent. 1976.
Evans, John and W. G. McNaught. *The School Music Teacher: a Guide to Teaching Singing in Schools by Tonic Sol-fa Notation and Staff Notation.* London: Curwen. 1923.
Fiddes, E. *Chapters in the History of Owens College and of Manchester University 1851–1914.* Manchester: University Press. 1937.
Fielden, Thomas. *The Science of Piano Technique.* London: Macmillan. 1927.
Findlay, J. J. *The Children of England: a Contribution to Social History and to Education.* London: Methuen. 1923.
Findlay, J. J. *Principles of Class Teaching.* London: Macmillan. 1930.
Galloway, William Johnson. *Musical England.* London: Christophers. 1910.
Gordon, Peter and Denis Lawton. *Curriculum Change in the Nineteenth and Twentieth Centuries.* London: Hodder and Stoughton. 1978.
Greer, David, editor. *Hamilton Harty: His Life and Music.* Belfast: Blackstaff Press. 1979.
Hallé, Charles. *The Autobiography of Charles Hallé with Correspondence and Diaries.* Edited by Michael Kennedy. London: Paul Elek. 1972.
Hartog, P. J., editor. *The Owens College, Manchester (Founded 1851): a Brief History of the College and Description of its Various Departments.* Manchester: Cornish. 1900.
Hey, Spurley. *Manchester's Educational Problem.* Manchester: Education Committee. 1918.
Hey, Spurley. *Notes on the Aim of Education in Elementary Schools.* Manchester: No publisher given. 1923.
Hey, Spurley. *Value for Money in Education.* Manchester: Hope. 1925.
Horrocks, Cyril R. *The Student's Guide to the Art of Teaching the Pianoforte.* London: Reeves. 1918.
Jacques-Dalcroze, Emile. *Rhythm, Music and Education.* Translated from the French by Harold F. Rubinstein. Woking: The Dalcroze Society (Inc.) 1967.
Jones, Lance G. E. *The Training of Teachers in England and Wales: a Critical Survey.* London: Oxford University Press. 1924.
Kennedy, Michael. *The Hallé Tradition: a Century of Music.* Manchester: University Press. 1960.
Kennedy, Michael. *The History of the Royal Manchester College of Music.* London: Oxford University Press. 1971.
Last, Joan. *The Young Pianist.* London: Oxford University Press. 1956.
Loesser, Arthur. *Men, Women and Pianos: a Social History.* New York: Simon and Schuster. 1954.

Bibliography

Mackerness, E. D. *A Social History of English Music.* London: Routledge and Kegan Paul. 1964.
Macpherson, Stewart. *Music and its Appreciation.* London: Joseph Williams. 1910.
Macpherson, Stewart. *The Musical Education of the Child.* London: Joseph Williams. 1915.
Maltby, S. E. *Manchester and the Movement for National Elementary Education 1800–1870.* Manchester: University Press. 1918.
Manchester Faces and Places. Volume 4. Manchester: Woodhead. 1893.
Manchester Faces and Places. Volume 16. Manchester: Woodhead. 1905.
Matthay, Tobias. *The Act of Touch in all its Diversity.* London: Longmans. 1903.
Matthay, Tobias. *The Visible and Invisible in Pianoforte Technique.* London: Oxford University Press. 1932.
Nettel, Reginald. *The Englishman Makes Music.* London: Dennis Dobson. 1952.
Parsons, R. G. *Birch-in-Rusholme: a Brief Account of the Church and its History.* Rusholme: Grayson. 1923.
Rainbow, Bernarr. *The Land Without Music: Musical Education in England 1800–1860 and its Continental Antecedents.* London: Novello. 1967.
Robert-Blunn, John. *Northern Accent: The Life Story of the Northern School of Music.* Altrincham: John Sherratt. 1972.
Roberts, Robert. *The Classic Slum.* Harmondsworth: Penguin. 1973.
Scholes, Percy A. *The Listener's Guide to Music.* London: Oxford University Press. 1919.
Scholes, Percy A. *Musical Appreciation in Schools: How – and Why?* London: Oxford University Press. 1920.
Scholes, Percy A. *Learning to Listen by Means of the Gramophone.* London: The Gramophone Company. 1921.
Scholes, Percy A. *Everybody's Guide to Broadcast Music.* London: Oxford University Press. 1925.
Scholes, Percy A. *Music, the Child and the Masterpiece.* London: Oxford University Press. 1935.
Scholes, Percy A. *The Mirror of Music 1844–1944.* London: Novello and Oxford University Press. 1947.
Selleck, R. J. W. *English Primary Education and the Progressives 1914–1939.* London: Routledge and Kegan Paul. 1972.
Simon, Brian. *Education and the Labour Movement 1870–1920.* London: Lawrence and Wishart. 1974.
Simon, E. D. *How the Manchester Education Committee Works.* Manchester: University Press. 1934.
Simpson, Kenneth, editor. *Some Great Music Educators.* London: Novello. 1976.
Sneyd-Kynnersley, E. M. *H.M.I. Some Passages in the Life of One of H.M. Inspectors of Schools.* London: Macmillan. 1908.
Stewart, W. A. C. *Progressives and Radicals in English Education 1750–1950.* London: Macmillan. 1972.
Taylor, Dorothy. *Music Now.* Milton Keynes: The Open University Press. 1979.
Walker, A. C. *The Contribution of Walter Carroll (1869–1955) to Music Education.* Unpublished M.Ed. thesis. University of Manchester. 1983.
Walker, Ernest. *A History of Music in England.* London: Oxford University Press. 1952.
Warriner, John. *Handbook on the Art of Teaching as Applied to Music for the Use of*

Bibliography

Students. London: Board of Trinity College. 1904.

Warriner, John, editor. *National Portrait Gallery of British Musicians.* London: Sampson Low, Marston. n.d.

Withers, Stanley. *The Royal Manchester College of Music.* Manchester: no publisher given. 1918.

Young, Percy M. *The Concert Tradition: From the Middle Ages to the Twentieth Century.* London: Routledge and Kegan Paul. 1965.